# ORGANIZATIONAL CHANGE:
## An Exploratory Study and Case History

# ORGANIZATIONAL CHANGE:

## An Exploratory Study and Case History

## by MICHAEL TUSHMAN

*ILR PAPERBACK No. 15*

*1974*

*NEW YORK STATE SCHOOL OF INDUSTRIAL AND LABOR RELATIONS*
*A Statutory College of the State University*
*CORNELL UNIVERSITY*

Price: Paper, $6.75

ORDER FROM
Publications Division
New York State School of Industrial and Labor Relations
Cornell University, Ithaca, New York 14850

Library of Congress Catalog Card Number: 73-620201
ISBN: 0-87546-055-0

SAMPLE CITATION: Michael Tushman, *Organizational Change: An Exploratory Study and Case History,* ILR Paperback No. 15 (Ithaca: New York State School of Industrial and Labor Relations, Cornell University, 1974).

PRINTED IN THE UNITED STATES OF AMERICA
BY HOFFMAN PRINTING COMPANY

To
Marilyn and My Family

# Contents

# Figure and Charts

# Acknowledgements

I wish to express my gratitude to the many teachers, colleagues, and friends who assisted in the preparation of this book. In retrospect, obligations for this kind of project become much clearer. Professor Leopold Gruenfeld was instrumental in the initiation, conceptualization, and further elaboration of this study. His intellectual stimulation and orientation to social science were a constant source of excitment and insight to me for this project in particular and my education in general. Professors Ned Rosen and William F. Whyte provided the combination of support, stimulation, and constraint necessary for the successful completion of the initial phase of this book. Dr. Alan Hundert greatly assisted me both in the field work and in the integration of the case, while the late Professor Donald Marquis provided me with critical comments that substantially improved the text.

This book has also been furthered by the stimulation, encouragement, and criticisms of my fellow graduate students while I was at Cornell University. My special thanks to Stuart Freedman and Michael McManus for being sounding boards and critics above and beyond the call of duty.

To all the men at Becket go my thanks and appreciation for providing me with such a rewarding experience. The openness, support, and enthusiastic cooperation made the research a real pleasure and added immeasurably to my graduate education.

Last, but most importantly, I must express my gratitude to my wife Marilyn; this book has truly been a joint project.

M.T.
1973

# Introduction

*"We are born in organizations, educated by organizations, and most of us spend much of our lives working for organizations. We spend much of our leisure time paying, playing, and praying in an organization and when the time comes for burial, the largest organization of them all — the state — must grant official permission" (Etzioni, 1964: 1).*

If we take Etzioni's statement seriously, then organizations certainly deserve study. While organizations as such have been studied intensively, the area of organizational change has received comparatively little systematic attention. The development of the systems perspective, along with the inclusion of external considerations such as the environment and technology, has advanced the organizational design literature (Woodward, 1965; Vroom, 1967; Lawrence and Lorsch; 1967); yet a gap has grown in the study of organizational change. While many books have been written on the relation of change to the design of organizations, "there are very few that provide a clue for the identification of strategic levers for [organizational] alteration. . . . They are theories of change and not theories of changing" (Bennis, 1966: 99). This study will be primarily concerned with this "changing" problem and will be directed at the problems and processes of planned organizational change.

If environments and technologies are indeed changing as rapidly as both essayists (Toffler, 1970; Gardner, 1965) and academicians (Thompson, 1967; Hage and Aiken, 1970; Bennis, 1963, 1966; and Lawrence and Lorsch, 1967) observe and if technology and the environments have important implications for effective organizational design, the processes and strategies of organizational change must be considered. The need for "theories of changing" has been further heightened by the recent United States Department of Health, Education and Welfare (1973) report, *Work in America,* which concludes that the present organization of work is inadequate. While the redesign of jobs is the "keystone of this report"

(United States Department of Health, Education and Welfare, 1973: xvii), job redesign and change cannot be done independently of organizational change. In all, then, the static models of organizational design are incomplete without a complementary model or theory of changing.

The reaction to the need for organizational change has been the development of largely independent change techniques. A review of the uses of behavioral science techniques by Lake and his associates (1969) describes a plethora of change packages on the market. The problem they describe, a description reinforced by Campbell (1971), Michael (1970), Taylor (1971), and Beer (in press), is that concentration on tool development has resulted in a neglect of the questions of how, what, why, or when of the various tools. What is missing is a theory of organizational change that will fit the extensive work on organizational design. In short, the static either-or orientations must be broadened to include problems of the dynamics of changing.

From this perspective the relevance of organizational change to the practitioner is clear. If technologies and environments (both internal and external) are changing for his organization and if the manager is bound by competitive constraints, he must be able to react and adapt to these changes. The problem of coping with the demands for change makes the area of organizational change and its development practically important.

This study contributes to the organizational change literature in two distinct ways. The case itself reports on a long-term change process in a small-sized manufacturing plant and traces the plant over a forty-two month period during which its management had to respond to a declining economy and increased outside competition. Longitudinal data form each of several phases; preinterventions, interventions, and postinterventions are reported. The process of change and the context within which the changes took place are presented in detail. Even though the study only used a sample of one, many possible insights on the processes and problems of change in a complex organization can be taken from the case. At a general level, this study goes beyond the case to develop some systematic ideas on organizational change. From the case and the review of the literature on organizations, a primitive model and a number of hypotheses on organizational change will be developed. More specifically, a contingency approach to organizational change will be elaborated on. Just as different organizations require different structures to be most effective (Lawrence and Lorsch, 1967), different organizations will also require different change strategies, as Chapter Three demonstrates. Thus, more generalizable statements can be induced from the case. These statements taken as a whole call for a more differentiated approach to the problem of organizational change.

In summary, this book will be directed at the problem and processes of planned organizational change from concrete and more general perspectives. Of particular concern here are questions of effective change strategies, the process of change, and theoretical propositions to link the diverse empirical work done on organizational change. While no attempt will be made to answer the problems and questions, a beginning will be made in the research process. The research here is exploratory and will not try to test hypotheses. The case study will trace the patterns of interaction within and between the functional areas of the plant. Other process-oriented variables, such as problem-solving ability, the recognition and confrontation of conflict, interpersonal relationships, and the presence or lack of a systems perspective in the plant, will also be described. Organizational variables such as productivity and sales figures will also be reported, not to test for differences over time, but rather to acquaint the reader with the background within which the case progressed.

CHAPTER 1

# ORGANIZATIONAL CHANGE: A REVIEW AND PERSPECTIVE

Even though published more than fifteen years ago, *The Dynamics of Planned Change* by Lippit, Watson, and Westley (1958) continues to be the foundation of much that is current in organizational change literature (Bennis, 1969; Schein, 1970; Beer, in press). In a wide-ranging discussion on the process of change, Lippit and his associates attempted to develop a general theory of change based on their notion of "planned change," which they define as a decision to make a deliberate effort to improve the system and to obtain the help of a change agent in making this improvement (Lippit *et al.,* 1958).

Based on the Lewinian tradition, Lippit and his coauthors conceive not of change, but of the process of change over time. The organization begins at state one and shifts to another and more effective dynamic equilibrium. The authors expand Lewin's three-step process of change into a five-phase process. Their revised process includes development of a need for change ("unfreezing"), establishment of a change relationship, working toward change ("moving"), stabilization of change ("freezing"), and achieving a terminal relationship (Lippit *et al.,* 1958).

The authors discuss all five phases, especially elaborating on the client-agent relationship. Of most importance to this study, though, is their third phase, the moving aspect of the change process. How does the change agent get effective leverage on the system? What change strategies are most effective for moving the organization? The development of a need for change and the establishment of a client-agent relationship will be assumed as given. The problems of stabilization and of achieving a terminal relationship are other real problems that will not be discussed here (see Beckhard, 1969; Hage and Aiken, 1970; Kolb, 1970). The problem to be considered in this study is one of leverage.

Lippit and his associates discuss the problem of choosing the most appropriate leverage point and to that end further break up their third phase into three subphases: diagnosing, establishing goals, and change efforts. While they emphasize the problem of leverage as the "keystone of the whole change process" (Lippit *et al.;* 1958: 139), their discussion goes no further. Thus, the authors completely describe the possibilities of planned change, even to the extent of suggesting proper educational programs for a change agent, yet leave unanswered the critical question of *how* the change is to be accomplished. Their most basic question on optimal change levers and strategies is posed, yet left unresolved. It is with these leverage and strategy questions that this study will be primarily concerned.

## APPROACHES TO ORGANIZATIONAL CHANGE

Conceptually, how can we arrive at other change strategies? Given the highly interdependent nature of organizations, the problem of change can easily become bewildering. Simplification becomes both desirable and inevitable. Leavitt (1965) has selected four interacting variables he terms task, technology, people, and structure. The task variable is seen as the primary output variable, while people, technology, and structure are seen as potential strategies for organizational change. In the systems tradition, Leavitt proposes the following interdependent system:

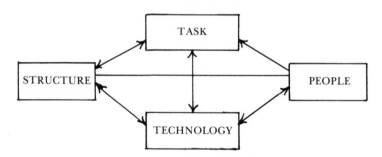

*Figure: Approaches to Organizational Change*

Harold J. Leavitt, "Applied Organizational Change in Industry: Structural, Technological and Humanistic Approaches," in James G. March (ed.); *Handbook of Organizations,* © 1965 by Rand McNally and Company, Chicago, p.1145. Reprinted by permission of Rand McNally College Publishing Company.

Each approach to organizational change differs in terms of points of entry, the primary lever of change, and the causal sequence of change (Leavitt, 1965).

From the literature to date, organizational change can be roughly divided into two areas. If Leavitt's analysis is used, one can be termed the *structural approach*, the other the *people approach*. Because they are very similar, what Leavitt terms technological and structural approaches to change will be considered together (Zaleznick, 1965; Barnes, 1967; Hornstein *et al.*, 1971, use similar schemes). In practice, the differences between the two approaches is less dramatic and areas of overlap confuse the analysis. For the sake of clarity, however, this chapter will deliberately highlight their basic differences in approaching organizational change.

While both approaches have produced a number of tools (Campbell *et al.*, 1970), all of these efforts have produced few systematic studies to report (Campbell, 1971; Barnes, 1967). For this reason the conceptual background of both schools will be studied. Research will be cited when available.

## STRUCTURAL APPROACHES

The structural school of thought can be traced to the scientific management and administrative science movements early in this century. Stimulated by F. W. Taylor and Henri Fayol, the scientific approach was directed at discovering the best way to organize. With their closed-system perspective, the thrust of organizational design was direct. One must only follow the rules of organizing and the question of organizational change need never come up (see Maisse, 1965). Since Mayo, the folly of the simplistic notions and confident principles of scientific management have been exposed. Scientific management did indeed work for certain kinds of organizations, but the principles were meant to apply to all organizations. This school's closed-system perspectives have been abandoned and a view emphasizing the organization in constant commerce with and potential dependence on its environment has taken its place (Thompson, 1967; Katz and Kahn, 1966).

An established structural perspective on organizational change is the work done by the interactionist school including Arensberg, Chapple, Homans, Sayles, and Whyte (Mouzelis, 1967). This school approaches social organizations in terms of patterns of activities, sentiments, and interactions. In a reaction to the psychologizing of traditional human relations, the interactionist concentrates on the frequency and duration of observable behaviors. As Chapple and Sayles (1961:136) say bluntly, "mysterious workings of the mind" must be seen as a result of behavior.

Chapple is representative of this school's perspective. His view is that one does not change attitudes and behaviors by teaching new skills, but rather by changing the interactional structure of the organization. Once this structure is changed, attitudes and performance will follow (Chapple and Sayles, 1961). Arensberg and Tootel (1957) and Sayles (1962) report evidence for this interactionist perspective. While Sayles admits to the use of conversion approaches to change behavior, this is clearly a secondary strategy. In terms of the time dimension important to this approach, Sayles elaborates a process of change including organizational checks on system stability, criteria for deviation evaluation, patterns of corrective action (that is, structural changes like work-flow shifts), and administrative action to validate the changes.

Change is thus seen as a continual process of structural adaptments (Sayles, 1962). Whyte (1951, 1971) takes a more moderate position and observes that interactions do lead to a change in sentiments, but then sentiments can create the conditions for further changes in interactions. Nevertheless, the primary lever in a dramatic change in union-management relations was a change in interaction patterns (Whyte, 1951). In a similar vein, combining interactionist and applied anthropology views, Holmberg (1960) and Whyte (1971) have traced the development of Peruvian communities in terms of patterns of interactions and the resultant changes in sentiments and activities.

Another structural orientation is more explicitly sociological. Perrow, Blau, Hage and Aiken, and Tausky are among the sociologists who are interested in organizational change. The sociological viewpoint considers the roles people play rather than the nature of personalities in these roles most important. Further, the organization is defined in terms of roles and role relationships. It follows that with this structural orientation, the levers of adjustment and change must be directed at role definitions, role relationships, and role behavior.

In an admittedly imperialistic essay, Perrow (1970) scolds those with the psychological bias that concentrates on the individual or on training programs. His "sociological position" is that training focuses on too small a picture, leaving out the effects of history, technology, the incentive structure, and the like (Perrow, 1970). Considering organizational change, Perrow is quite explicit. He cites an example of how some treatment-oriented (through training) prison guards become custodial because of prison rules, structure, and technique. Using other examples, he concludes that behavioral and attitudinal change can best be brought about by devices such as rules, role prescriptions, and reward structures (Perrow, 1970). A more recent essay by Perrow continues and elaborates on his sociological view of organizations and goes much further in explicating the sociological position and comparing it to what he terms "the human relations model" (Perrow, 1972). While Hage and Aiken (1970) are less chauvanistic about the sociological approach than Perrow, their analysis of change efforts and innovation is just as strictly couched in sociological terms.

The structuralists' assumptions about the individual are quite definite. In order to work at the structural level of analysis, they make certain assumptions about the central tendencies of aggregates. Individuals as role occupants are considered constant. Thus, in the interactions of two managers, the structuralist considers the two individuals filling roles which are tied to and defined by patterned activities within their organization. This perspective minimizes the psychological aspects of any social situation.

Since Taylor and Fayol the structural orientation has treated organizations as interdependent systems embedded in an uncertain environment. While sentiments, interactions, and activities are acknowledged as primary variables, the structuralists agree that influencing the patterns of interaction is the most effective change strategy. Besides the research already mentioned, examples of research (mostly field studies) taking a structural approach to change include Lawrence (1958), Guest (1962), Morse and Reimer (1956), Blau (1955), Golembiewski (1964), Steele (1971), and Liebow (1967).

The examples cited make a convincing case for the structural approach. While this macroapproach undoubtly contains major truths, they have yet to be consistently explicated. Further, a few structural interventions which were less successful will be discussed later. The problem then becomes when, and under what conditions, does structural change lead to desired behavioral and organizational change? What are the effects of differing environments and technologies and of group influence and individual predispositions on the process of change? These questions remain to be cleared up before a more comprehensive approach to organizational change can be elaborated.

## PEOPLE APPROACHES

The other major approach to organizational change is what Leavitt calls the people approach. Other similar terms currently used in the literature include power equalization (Leavitt, 1965; Shepard, 1965; Strauss, 1964), eupsychian management (Maslow, 1965), planned change (Barnes, 1967; Lippit et al., 1958), organizational renewal (Lippit, 1969), and participation (Likert, 1961, 1967; Mann and Neff, 1961). All refer to a set of efforts to effect organizational change through changes in people. These people approaches attempt to change organizations by first influencing attitudes, values, and norms. Structure is believed to follow. While usually aware of technological and structural constraints, these researches are mainly preoccupied with people as the primary lever for change.

Since the classic work by Lewin (1958) on changing food habits and Coch and French's study (1948) in a pajama factory, much work has been done on behavioral approaches to change. In fact, as Leavitt (1965) notes, most of the research on organizational change over the past fifteen years has been heavily people oriented. While the results remain change in interpersonal and intergroup relation (just as with the structuralists), the primary lever is through what Shepard terms reeducation (Shepard, 1965). The major aim of reeducation is to provide participants with a new cognitive framework for viewing interpersonal and intergroup relations and at the same time to build a set of collaborative relations among task-interdependent participants.

The people orientation with its emphasis on reeducation has over the past few years taken on a new label, organizational development. Although there are many definitions of organizational development in the literature (Kegan, 1971), a representative definition can be taken from Bennis (1969:10): ". . . it is an *educational strategy* adopted to bring about a planned organizational change" [Emphasis added]. While specific strategies might differ, organizational development always concentrates on values, attitudes, and organizational climate. The general organizational development strategy attempts to move the organization from what Shepard and Blake (1962) term a mechanical system to an organic system. Mechanical systems are characterized by authority-obedience relationships, centralized decision making, and the avoidance of conflict. Organic systems have the opposite characteristics. While both systems are abstractions, the basic idea is that more organic organizations are better able to adapt and change to environmental and technical changes than are mechanistic organizations. Argyris talks about similar conditions calling them World A and World B (Argyris, 1969). While the variables considered important and the ends desired are similar, there are great differences in the choice of programs used to implement a reeducational change program (Back, 1972).

Organizational development has grown rapidly over the past decade (French and Bell, 1973), but only two approaches will be discussed here. Others not included are systematic feedback (Heller, 1970; Beckhard, 1969), process consultation (Schein, 1969), organizational renewal (Lippit, 1969), and a series of organizational development and training programs developed and run by the National Training Laboratory Institute for Applied Behavioral Science (Weschler and Schein, 1962).

ARGYRIS: Argyris (1957, 1962, 1964, 1965, 1971, 1973) has developed an organizational development model based on the notion of interpersonal competence and its relationship to organizational effectiveness. Because of its similarity in both conceptual outlook and action orientation to other organizational development efforts and because Argyris has developed and tested his model further than most, it will be described at length.

Basic to Argyris' model is the lack of fit between the individual and the typical organization. Following the influence of Carl Rogers, Argyris makes a number of assumptions regarding human personality, including a development from passivity to activity and from dependence to independence and a development from lack of awareness of self to an awareness and control over self.

This model implies a developmental growth process inherent in each individual. Healthy adults then strive towards the fulfillment of activity, independence, and control needs. Also critical to individual growth is the kind and quality of interpersonal relationships encountered by the individual. Argyris hypothesizes that a critical source of psychological life and human growth is from authentic relationships. "Authentic relationships are those relationships in which the individual enhances his sense of self and other-awareness in such a way that others can do the same" (Argyris, 1962:21). He further states that authentic relationships will increase as the following increase: giving and receiving nonevaluative feedback; openness to new values, attitudes, and feelings; and the ability to take risks. Authentic relationships create the conditions for interpersonal competence among the individuals involved. Thus, interpersonal competence, through authentic relationships, is hypothesized to be essential for individual (and later, organizational) growth (Argyris, 1962).

Argyris also has definite notions of organizations as strategies designed to achieve certain objectives. To this end, he sees organizations as being rational and specialized and containing specified communication patterns. In the traditional organization, Argyris believes, employees work where they have little control, they are expected to be passive, and they are expected to produce under conditions leading to psychological failure (Argyris, 1957). These conditions lead to a negation of both human growth and interpersonal competence.

Comparing individual needs for authentic relations and the organizational needs of rationality and order, Argyris notes a basic incongruence between the two. More than that, he hypothesizes that the incongruence increases as employees become more mature or as the job becomes more mechanized. In short, Argyris concludes that formal organizational values, if followed, create a social system in which the members' interpersonal competence must decrease. This he terms the organizational dilemma (Argyris, 1964). The results of this decrease in organizational competence are external commitment, conformity, mistrust, ineffective decision making, and organizational rigidity. Further, Argyris

(1962) notes that these all feed back on each other, resulting in an ineffective organization.

Given this conceptual scheme and the way the problem is phrased, the organizational change strategy is obvious, improve interpersonal competence. Argyris (1962:53) is quite explicit about this

> ... the appropriate influence is in the direction of increasing interpersonal competence. Although *increasing interpersonal competence is a necessary first step,* ... basic changes will require a modification of technological factors also. The interpersonal factors, however, should come first, closely followed by the others [Emphasis added].

The implication is that traditional organizational forms can be adapted and changed so that interpersonal competence can be effected throughout the organization. In this vein, Argyris (1957:211) talks about a fusion process by which both the individual and organization "simultaneously obtain maximum self actualization."

The question of how and in what directions this "newer form of organization" should be organized is discussed at length in terms of a mix model (Argyris, 1964). The question that we are interested in is not what to develop (organizational design), but how the change takes place.

Argyris's change strategy is based on laboratory (T group) methods. His initial emphasis is on the top-level management, but the program as a whole must eventually involve the entire organization (Argyris, 1964). Broadly speaking, there are three steps involved in the change process. They are similar in format to Lewin's notions.

The first step is organizational diagnosis. The process of diagnosis provides both the client and the agent an opportunity for learning about the dynamics of the system. Processes usually concentrated on include decision making, conflict resolution, and goal setting. The next step usually consists of a laboratory program. The objectives of the laboratory program according to Argyris are to help participants modify their values towards increasing the quality of feedback and to decrease dependence, conformity, and organizational defenses. The lab is often, but not always, directed at problems uncovered in the diagnostic phase of the change. It is essentially conceived of as a learning experience. Given these new skills, the third step is for management to intervene and set an example for the rest of the organization.

Argyris (1962, 1964) has reported a number of field experiences in business, research, and governmental organizations. While Harrison (1962) has documented some transfer problems, Argyris (1962, 1964, 1965, 1971) reports that his model was helpful in diagnosis, evaluation, and action implementation. Many others have reported successful use of laboratory training in organizational change including Golembiewski and Carrigan (1970), Winn (1969), Rubin (1967), Beckhard (1969), and Schein and Bennis (1965).

BLAKE AND MOUTON: The planned change orientation advocated by Argyris and many others (Winn, 1969; Shepard, 1965; Kegan, 1971) emphasizes reeducation. While the term employed is organizational change, much of the literature has only dealt with direct change induction of small groups (Campbell *et al.*, 1970). The logic is that this group (usually top management) will then effect organizationwide renewal. A broader attack on the problem has been developed by Blake and Mouton (1964).

Moving between business, government, and academia, Blake and Mouton have developed an organizational development program they call the managerial grid. They note the organizational problem posed by Argyris, but their solution is different. Rather than talk in terms of some fusion processes that maximize individual and organizational needs, they conceive of "concern for people" and "concern for production" as two independent variables. In this way, both can, conveniently, be simultaneously maximized.

With these two dimensions, Blake and Mouton form a simple grid with concern for people the vertical axis and concern for production the horizontal axis. On the basis of this twofold framework, they locate five types of managerial strategies ranging from country club (1,1) to team management style (9,9). Each strategy has its set of assumptions relating to people and production. Each constitutes another way of thinking, culminating in the 9,9 approach (Blake and Mouton, 1964).

The grid program has been worked out to the last detail and is sold as a prepackaged development program designed to be taught and applied by line managers over a period of six phases and at least three years. The program is self-administered except for occasional consultation when desired.

Briefly the six phases are
Phase One:    Structured learning laboratory with one week away from the plant in which interpersonal education is emphasized;
Phase Two:    Team building within functional groups;
Phase Three:  Interteam building with work towards integration between functional groups;
Phase Four:   Goal setting for the organization;

Phase Five:   Goal implementation;

Phase Six:   Stabilization of changes and a continuing monitoring of progress.

The six phases can be divided into two major programs. The first two phases make up the first part and involve management development. The grid helps the participants to develop a language system for describing their current managerial styles and provides an ideal to work towards, 9,9. The last four phases are designed to prod the managers, through team development and critique, to work toward the 9,9 goals of organizational excellence.

Each stage is worked out in great detail, especially the week-long laboratory. Anxiety is minimized by the high degree of structure and the task orientation throughout. In its emphasis on two to three years of follow-up, the grid formalizes a procedure that takes advantage of long-term monitoring and feedback of progress.

In all, with its structure and its emphasis on the whole organization participating, the grid program counteracts many of the T group's shortcomings and goes beyond the small group bias of many of the people approaches. Even so, the direction of change is the same. Through the learning of openness, participation, and conflict resolution, cognitive and attitudinal change is hypothesized to yield overall organizational change.

Besides that of Blake and Mouton, there have been very few research reports on the grid process. The results are impressive as reported in a field study by Blake *et al.* (1964), an intermediate evaluation by Beer and Kleisath (1967), and a field experiment by Kreinik and Colarelli (1971). While not reported in the literature, Barnes (1967) notes many other large-scale organizational efforts based on grid concepts that indirectly support the program. Even so, with all the writing about and intervening with the grid concepts, the amount of reportable literature on grid-oriented organizational change is less than meager (Campell, 1971; Campbell *et al.,* 1970).

Like the structuralists, the people-approach supporters spin a convincing web. Greiner (1967) is a good example. He sought to identify the conditions that differentiate successful from less successful change efforts and found that all of the successful efforts involved what he termed a shared approach to change (power equalization). The less successful ones did not use the shared approach. His conclusion was that successful organizational change depends on improvements in interpersonal relationships and concomitant redistribution of power towards a more shared situation.

*10*

The problem with Greiner's review is twofold. First, it is definitional in nature. His definition of shared power is so wide that it encompasses both structural (Guest, 1962; Lawrence, 1958) and people (Mann and Neff, 1961) approaches under the same label. In effect, both approaches are combined in the same term. A second problem, and this omission is typical of the people approaches, is that he pays no attention to the kinds of organizations studied and their relevant environments. This is the complementary error to the structural fallacy mentioned before. Thus, factors involved with organizational size, structure, technology, and environment are systematically ignored by the people-approach advocates. If not ignored, structural factors are assumed constant, an assumption not tenable today (Thompson, 1966). In this vein, Katz and Kahn (1966:391) observe: "This [the individual approach] is not so much an illogical proposition as it is an oversimplification which neglects the interrelatedness of people in an organizational structure."

Like the structural approach, the people orientation is right, but not right enough. We have learned from scientific management that the "one best way" approach is inadequate. While much empirical work has been done on training groups and educational strategies (Campbell *et al.*, 1970), very little has been done on systematic organizational change. The analytical work, while extensive, has systematically ignored a number of questions. For instance, what organizational structures, or environments, permit the behavioral-structural link specified by the people approach? What are the implications of differing task requirements for organizational change? The arguments regarding whether structure or education is the best approach have generated much rhetoric, yet very little research or theory to date, and have not furthered a more systematic approach to change. The question should shift from whether either one is best to when and under what conditions combinations of structural and behavioral interventions lead to effective organizational change. What is needed is both a more systematic conceptual outlook and an increase in more systematic change research.

## A WIDER PERSPECTIVE

To this point structural and people (educational) approaches have been discussed at some length. Each view has been criticized for biases (sociological or psychological) and each has been presented with only supportive research results. As might be expected, the verdict from the available research makes this either-or approach too simplistic.

The work of Trist and Bamforth (1951), Rice (1958), and others from the Tavistock Institute presents real problems to the structural perspective. This socio-technical school has reported field studies from England

and India clearly showing that both technical and social factors must be considered simultaneously for effective organizational change. In a number of cases the Tavistock researchers found that the same structural change had very different effects depending on the kind of social system permitted. The lesson for organizational change is that any structural change must be evaluated with how it fits into and affects the social system. Gouldner's (1954) gypsum plant study illustrates the same point.

The people approaches, with their simplistic structural notions, have also been criticized. Buchanan (1969), Friedlander (1967), and Cadwell (1970) stress that training alone is not an effective organizational change lever. Further, a number of empirical studies undertaken to evaluate behavioral interventions have yielded equivocal results at best (Campbell and Dunnette, 1968; Harrison, 1962; Back, 1972). Harrison documented the lack of transfer from a training lab to the home organization. He explained the lack in terms of structural constraints on the new behaviors back at the home organization. Other uncertain or negative results have been reported by Cadwell (1970), Bowers (1973), Campbell (1971), and Leavitt (1965) and summarized by Campbell and Dunnette (1968). The general conclusion reached by Beer and Huse (1972), Beer (in press), Cadwell (1970), and Buchanan (1969) is that, while behavioral change is necessary, it must be part of a multilever approach to change.

Both approaches to organizational change have shown conditional success. Neither can substantiate itself as the best approach under all conditions. The literature to date, almost by default, suggests that some combination, some sequence of approaches, may be a more effective way to approach the problem of change. A more general approach would necessarily include *both structural* and *behavioral* interventions. The most appropriate combination would depend on the organizational task and environmental givens. The implication is that there are more effective ways of introducing and carrying through change depending on the organization. Taylor (1971), Beer and Huse (1972), and Seashore and Bowers (1963, 1970) have reported studies that support this dual strategy for change. This approach makes the intervention strategy a dependent variable.

This same conclusion can be reached from a more theoretical approach. Katz and Kahn (1966) use the concept of role to synthesize the typically disparate sociological and psychological approaches to organization. They write (p. 171): "[ role] is at one end of the building block of social systems and the summation of requirements with which the system confronts the individual member." In that light, role theory with its notions of role definition, focal person, role behavior, and set role takes into account what the individual brings to that role, the influence of members in the role set, and the influence of the role system. Further, a number of theorists (Weick, 1969; Katz and Kahn, 1966; Taylor, 1971; Shimmin, 1971) have conceptualized organizations in terms of role relationships or as role systems.

If this role-oriented definition of organizations is taken seriously, organizational change must be conceptualized in terms of changing the patterns of interactions. It follows, given the definition of role systems, that studying and implementing organizational change must take into account the individual and structural approaches and the interaction of the two (Pugh, 1966; Kahn, *et al.*, 1964).

In addition to conceptualizing organizations as role systems, much recent literature has emphasized the critical importance of technology and environment in organizational design (Thompson, 1967; Katz and Kahn, 1966; Lawrence and Lorsch, 1967). In open-systems theory, the organization is influenced by variables at both its input and output stages and as such is faced with uncertainty. The central problem for organizations is coping with this uncertainty. If technologies and environments are major sources of uncertainty (Perrow, 1970) these differences must result in differences both in organizational design and in *organizational change strategies.* Perrow (1970:19) notes, ". . . today organizations come in great variety and . . . organizational theory must be varied to be useful." The same ought to hold true for theories of organizational change; they must be able to respond to organizational variability. The implication is that the change theorist must broaden his perspective to include both technological requirements and environmental constraints as they pertain to the problem of organizational change.

The ideas of role theory and open-systems theory each have direct implications for the study of organizational change. Role theory stresses the need for an integrated sociological and psychological perspective, an interdisciplinary approach to change. It implies that neither perspective is sufficient alone, but that *multiple levers* must be used to conceptualize and induce organizational change. Open-systems theory demands a more differentiated approach to change. Because of the multiplicity of organizational technologies and environment, no one best approach is justifiable. Organizational interventions must fit with technological and environmental givens (Lawrence and Lorsch, 1970). This fact then suggests the potential for a contingency approach to organizational change.

While the literature on this dual approach to change is scarce, the above discussion suggests, empirically and theoretically, that the combination of structural and behavioral interventions is a more general and more comprehensive approach to change. The second chapter of this study will trace the development of a small (500 employees) industrial plant.

*13*

The aim of this case study will be to conceptualize the many changes in terms of structural and behavioral interventions that took place over forty-two months. While the field study will not be a test of any change scheme, it can lend credence to the dual approach discussed above and stimulate further hypotheses on the process of organizational change.

# CHAPTER 2

# CASE STUDY

This chapter will trace the history of an industrial plant, Becket, over a span of three-and-one-half years, from January 1968 to August 1971. In order to aid in conceptualizing the change process occurring at the plant the chapter will be divided into four distinct stages:

January 1968-January 1970, Jake Mitchell as plant manager, immediate history;

January 1970-April 1970, Doug Freeman as plant manager, structural changes;

April 1970-March 1971, response to changes;

April 1971-August 1971, behavioral changes.

Within each stage, the interdepartment and intradepartment dynamics, the influence of the plant manager and his staff, economic conditions facing the plant, and general systemic plant variables will be described. The inclusion of the period 1968 to 1970 should add the historical background Greiner (1967, 1972) and Weick (1969) deem essential for obtaining the whole developmental perspective. There is, however, a danger in "taking snapshots" of social systems. A snapshot is static while Becket was constantly in flux. While this approach does, therefore, have aspects of unreality, as a whole it should preserve the dynamic nature of the conditions which were present (see Guest, 1962).

Becket is one plant of one division in the Boise Company. At Boise the divisions are decentralized and the plants operate freely within division constraints. Becket's plant manager, therefore, had a free hand to run the plant as he saw fit.

Becket is a glass production plant. While this necessarily makes the *manufacturing* group the largest and most influential area in the plant, the two other functional areas cannot be neglected. The *staff* group at Becket encompasses the purchasing, scheduling, and accounting functions and the *engineering* area's responsibilities lie in industrial, process, and development engineering subgroups.

An organizational list of personnel will be helpful. Only department-level managers will be noted; the lower-level managers will be identified as needed. The men in charge before Freeman (the new plant manager) took over are in parentheses: plant manager (Jake Mitchell), Doug Freeman; manufacturing, Bob Smith; staff (Paul Winters), Bob Mazur; comptroller, Mike McCall; engineering, John Brown; personnel manager, Frank O'Connor; business manager, George Brooks. (All names included here are fictitious.)

Because of the dynamic nature of the plant, the staff, engineering, and manufacturing areas cannot be simply described here. While manufacturing did change over the period, its basic technology did not. The technology at Becket was routine yet required skill in varying degrees. The manufacturing floor is divided in both function and area into the "hot and cold ends" of the plant.

The hot end consists of various hot operations which form, shape, and temper the glassware. No glass is made at Becket. The basic glass inputs, or blanks, are produced at other Boise facilities. The hot end is all male and each employee has a great deal of experience and skill with glass. Within the hot end the hierarchy of jobs goes from the relatively low-skilled cutters to the highest-skilled (and highest-paid) lampworkers. In the lamp section most work is made up of one-of-a-kind specials, while the other areas in the hot end turn out relatively standard stock items in batches typically no less than twenty-five. Lampworker or not, most men in the hot end work by hand and use machines as tools. All of the work in this area is done on a piece-rate system.

After a piece of glassware finishes its hot-end processes, it is transferred to the cold end where it is finished, stained, packed, and "sent out the door." As many people work in the cold end as in the hot, but there are women in the cold end. In general the work is more standardized and mechanized and requires relatively less skill than the work in the hot end. Much less of the work done here is on piece rate.

Until late in 1971, the technology in the plant was stable; most of the processes, techniques, and methods had been carried down from the past. While the hot end required more skill than the cold end, both areas required skilled handwork. Nevertheless, the work to be done was predictable, certain, and, except for the lamp area, repetitive in proportion to the run length.

During the period of this study, Becket's task environment, which includes the input and output sides of the organization, changed in a number of respects. Becket's input side is largely controlled by Boise since the basic inputs are glass blanks. Besides these blanks, other inputs, such as decals, packaging, and machines, are purchased from other firms.

While the input side is not entirely certain, it presents few problems. The output side is more problematical. Becket has no sales group. The plant relies on the work of a divisional sales force. Most of Becket's products are standard catalogue items, yet specials make up 20 percent of its volume. Output goals are established to keep the salesmen supplied with a full inventory of standard items and to respond quickly on specials. The specials make both the input and output sides uncertain since these orders cannot be planned for in advance. During the period studied, competition became more respectable and a source of concern, especially with the decrease in Becket's orders starting in the 1970s. In addition to competition, the declining economy also affected the company. The volume was very susceptible to governmental and educational spending, and both areas cut back during the period under study. In all, the output side of Becket was increasingly uncertain.

## JANUARY 1968 TO JANUARY 1970: BECKET'S IMMEDIATE HISTORY

During the period 1968 to 1970 the economic picture facing Becket changed dramatically. From 1966 to 1968 plant sales and dollar volume continued to climb to reach the highest levels in the company's history. During this extended period of economic expansion, which began in the early 1960s, the plant increased in size and reached a high of over 600 employees by January 1968. In 1968 this steady progress was reversed; orders began to decline. As a result, plant sales and dollar volume decreased or at least did not increase through January 1970. To make matters worse, a number of glass products developed and made at Becket were transferred to other Boise plants where they could be made more cheaply. In short, the boom enjoyed by the plant throughout the 1960s had disappeared as the general United States economy took a turn for the worse. The response at Becket to this turnaround in the market was sluggish. Constrained by a slow and lazy plant culture, Becket's productivity record suffered. By the end of 1969 the rate of increase was 1.5 percent, the lowest in five years, even though the number of hourly employees had decreased, bringing the total plant level to 479 employees (see Appendix One, Chart A1).

PLANT MANAGER: The plant manager wields the power at Becket. From 1968 to 1970 the plant manager was Jake Mitchell who had previously been the production superintendent. Michell had his own style for running the plant and his idiosyncracies showed in many ways. Most important about Mitchell's reign was his relationship with the workers and the union, his experience with the manufacturing department, and his general orientation towards the climate of a manufacturing organization.

Mitchell was seen as a "nice guy" throughout the plant. He maintained contact with as many people as possible by making frequent tours of the plant and by always keeping his office door, on the main corridor, open. Mitchell had a particularly close relationship with the hourly workers and, consequently, the union at Becket. His relation with the union was termed congenial. In the evenings, he would often be found "guzzling the suds with the guys [from the manufacturing floor]. . . ." During Mitchell's term the union had direct influence on plant policy and established a number of formal and informal agreements with management. When Mitchell took over as plant manager, he failed to differentiate his new role from his old one of production superintendent to the extent that Bob Smith, his replacement as superintendent, was not given full responsibility for the operations of the floor. As was noted by a few men, "Bob was not the boss of the floor while Mitchell was the plant manager. . . ." Mitchell knew the floor and its problems and took a major hand in directing week-to-week operations. As if to emphasize this, his office and Smith's office were moved into the same area where they shared a secretary. Mitchell was strongly convinced of the overriding importance of manufacturing to Becket's success. As a result the staff and engineering areas were relatively neglected in budgets and influence in plant decisions. To the rest of the plant Mitchell was a "relaxed plant manager" who created a relaxing feeling of security and comfort with the employees. During the period of increasing sales and plant expansion his orientation produced no real problems.

MANUFACTURING: During Mitchell's stay as plant manager, the manufacturing group was by far the largest and most influential area in the plant. With the support and ear of the plant manager, the manufacturing men had the only real influence and were "quite used to getting their own way. . . ." The manufacturing department had seven department heads, including maintenance, and twenty-five shift foremen. Bob Smith was the production superintendent although most of his authority was taken by Mitchell. Mitchell met with the manufacturing department heads at least twice a week and made many operating decisions without Smith. The relationships within and between departments on the floor were poor. The cooperation and integration was extremely competitive and of a win or lose variety. Especially poor were the relations between the shift foremen and their respective department heads. The typical complaint was that the department head infringed on the responsibilities and duties of the shift foremen. Also, if for no other reason than size, the manufacturing area was very inefficient and confused. Lack in monitoring the flow of material by the staff group contributed to this confusion. In short, the manufacturing area was very large, unchecked by a staff function, directed by two managers not necessarily in concert, and, because of these conditions and internal conflicts, less efficient than possible.

ENGINEERING AND STAFF: Under the leadership of Mitchell, the manufacturing area was of primary importance and all other groups were looked on as helpers. The engineering department, although existing on paper and alive in body, was essentially not functioning at Becket. Engineering had no status, no purpose, a tiny budget, and, even, no parking spaces for department heads. The engineers fulfilled plantwide expectations and were known as "not a second- but a *third*-rate team." Their only activities were to "fight fires" on the floor, (handle sudden breakdowns), make sure the machines were kept in order, and take care of the piece-rate system. The engineers were looked at with disdain, especially by the manufacturing department, and were able to get little cooperation when needed. Late in 1969 John Brown, the new manager, arrived but his effect was not felt until after 1970. From 1968 to 1970 no new projects or process modifications were made at Becket. The prevailing ethic was noted by an engineer, "as long as business was good and we satisfied our customers, then everything was OK. . . ." This short time perspective and the total lack of technological considerations had real effects on the plant's ability to stay competitive. It was during these years that Becket began to face major outside competition.

Purchasing and scheduling were at the call of manufacturing and therefore their time perspectives were week to week at best. Because of the overriding influence of manufacturing and the absence of long-range goals, the planning function was, in fact not planning, but rather, management by crisis with the manufacturing men often defining the crisis. As observed: "Planning was nearsighted . . . rather than planning and forecasting they flew by the seat of their pants." The order of influence was manufacturing to staff, rarely the reverse.

Becket's immediate economic past was excellent and its environment was stable and predictable. With orders and sales high, Becket reached its largest size, 600 employees, during 1967. The economic success brought on fatness and inefficiency which, as will be seen, caused severe shock when conditions were forced into line. During this time Becket was in essence one large group, manufacturing; staff and engineering were second-order considerations. From the hourly and union point of view, Becket was a secure place to work. From a management perspective business was fine, and there was no perceived movement to change operating procedures. Problems were settled just enough to get by and the status quo was actively maintained. As was noted by Ben Morse, a department manager, "the good conditions actually encouraged inefficiency, sloppiness, and overall laziness. . . ." By early 1970 Becket had made no response to its newfound environment. It was in reality living in the past.

## JANUARY 1970 TO APRIL 1970

These four months brought many changes to Becket. February 1970 was a turning point in Becket's current history. Mitchell was promoted to a corporate position and Doug Freeman, "the golden boy," was promoted to plant manager. Freeman was a star in the Boise system. His background is instructive because it gives a feel for some of the cultural norms of Boise and explains why Boise people acted deferentially toward Freeman.

Freeman's family was from Boise and his father was a long and dedicated hourly employee. The younger Freeman grew up in Boise and after high school, where he was valedictorian, he entered Harvard University. At Harvard he was quarterback for the football team. After graduation and a stay in the Navy, Doug went to the Tuck School of Business at Dartmouth. After Tuck he was hired by Boise where in a relatively short time he progressed from shift foreman to department head and then to plant manager at three separate Boise plants. This progression all adds up to a perfect pedigree for Boise. He was seen by all as one "destined for bigger things." Becket was Freeman's biggest challenge to date. The plant was given to him with the mandate to make it meet a more ambitious budget; other than that direction, Freeman was unencumbered by his boss and the plant was his.

After a short time at Becket, Freeman made some basic decisions. Becket was to change. Freeman faced six problems: (A) Becket needed more business. Becket was totally dependent on orders from the outside and economic conditions did not look encouraging. Some way had to be found to increase sales volume at the plant. (B) There were no long-term plans and goals for Becket. As was noted before, the plant lived from period to period and was dominated by the myopic manufacturing area. (C) An engineering program was lacking. Over the previous four years the engineering program had accomplished nothing in the way of advancing the processes or technology at the plant. (D) Becket was not cost conscious. Along with the surplus of monthly and hourly employees was a lulling sense of security with a resultant increase in inefficiency. (E) There were communication and coordination problems all over the plant. (F) Finally, union influence at Becket was too great. Freeman's initial reaction was that the union was a major factor in Becket's poor operations and slowness to respond.

Given these problems Freeman was quick to initiate changes as well as the philosophy of change at Becket. He was constantly on the lookout for change opportunities. Difficult questions were asked at all levels, and employees were forced to justify techniques and methods in terms of "contributing to the Becket till." Each question explicitly asked "Is there a better way, how can we reduce costs . . . ?"

Affecting all further interventions was the establishment of five-year and one-year goals. These long-term goals were in answer to the question "what should we be planning for?" Freeman and his top team got together over a three month period to establish broad goals and to set criteria to evaluate Becket's performance. Although these goals were made by the group, the influence of Freeman cannot be underestimated. At least six goals were established: (A) The importance of the engineering department was to be increased. Automation and on-line processes were deemed crucial if Becket was to remain competitive. (B) New products would be developed. (C) Problem-solving techniques, especially at the lower managerial levels, would be increased. (D) Union influence would decrease. (E) Becket would be a more "flexible and vital organization." (F) Becket would become an example for the Boise company, especially in the Boise area. There is no coincidence in the similarity between the problems defined by Freeman and these goals. Thus, Becket's time perspective was raised from a period-to- period orientation to a more planned long-term view.

An immediate result of these planning sessions was the establishment of a "supervisor of business development." In response to the decrease in orders from the traditional markets, Freeman promoted George Brooks from comptroller to this new position. Brooks reported directly to Freeman. His task was to get new business to Becket by translating Becket's capabilities and potential into new glass areas and products. His domain was to be both inside Boise and outside; his measure of success, the amount of new business. Brooks was, in essence, a one-man sales department responsible only for Becket. Besides the goals and Brooks' new position a number of other changes were initiated by Freeman and his team. They can best be described by discussing each department separately.

ENGINEERING: As mentioned before, the engineering department at Becket was almost an apparition, there in fact but not in results. The change in engineering must be traced not only to Freeman's arrival but also to the promotion of John Brown to plant engineer late in 1969.

Brown was to engineering what Freeman was to Becket: change. Brown was hired late in Mitchell's stay to put some life into a failing department (it was not clear whether Mitchell or headquarters initiated this change). With the arrival of Freeman and the goals of the five-year plan, the importance of engineering was further reinforced. To Brown, the increased emphasis on engineering gave him and his area the responsibility for developing new machines, new processes, new techniques, and, in general, for keeping Becket up with the state of the art in glass technology. This task assumed even greater importance given the engineering void of the previous four years. To this end, Brown made great changes in the department.

Brown wanted to force his men to think in terms of the future and of saving money in the long run through modernization. With these considerations in mind the "project concept" was initiated. The department met and over a few weeks discussed projects for each area. Each manager, although pressured to take risks, worked out plans for his area's undertaking. Brown emphasized the risk factor by frequently noting that "anyone who is 100 percent successful has failed to stick his neck out. . . ." Projects were then written up and defined with goals, project value, method of measurement, and program spelled out in precise detail. While old maintenance and firefighting duties remained, Brown unilaterally redefined the time ratios to 80 percent on projects and 20 percent for maintenance work. His position was that the ability to fix problems on the floor was independent of an engineer's presence. By April, although under pressure, each engineer was working on his own self-defined project besides having his old firefighting responsibilities.

Another, more subtle, change brought by Brown was an emphasis on engineers as "special people." To Brown, an engineer ought to expect to work very hard. He was a professional with responsibility to his field and to Boise. Brown's notion of career revolved around this project concept. With each completed project the engineer advanced in his Boise career and gained in job security. Brown realized the potential for casualties in the department, but he was determined to create the best engineering section in Boise. Career development through sacrifice and hard work and the new professional philosophy espoused by Brown were very new factors in the engineering area.

Consistent with this tough philosophy and the project concept was the evaluation system initiated by Brown. The system was simple: either a project was completed as scheduled or it was not. "No excuses were accepted besides acts of God." Although Brown was approachable, was open to suggestions, and encouraged individual ideas on the formulation side of the project, he took no excuses on the output side. "Brown firmly believed that you could make good excuses for any poor result." Once a project was laid out, no excuses were accepted as valid. Brown too was evaluated by this method. Besides this "100 percent evaluation system" he and his men were evaluated in two other ways. Most importantly, the engineering department as a whole, and each engineer, was evaluated in terms of dollar volume contributed to Becket. If both levels could not show real contributions then direct sanctions, either replacements or layoffs, would take place. The men were also evaluated in terms of their problem-solving ability. This criterion, although applied to the uniqueness of projects, was more a consideration in firefighting abilities. With the shift in emphasis from floor work to project work, the engineer was expected to be able to resolve fires quickly and to keep them from arising. Further, if manufacturing floor time could not be kept down, project time would necessarily be reduced.

Another change in the engineering group was the inclusion of quality control under the engineering manager where before the quality control manager reported to Mitchell. The quality control group was relatively large (twenty-three inspectors). The men were dispersed throughout the plant to inspect the glassware as it was worked on during the many manufacturing stages. As a manufacturing man sarcastically observed: "They [quality control] flooded the floor. . . ." An informal study was carried out by Brown and Freeman in the belief that Becket was "quality happy." Their hypothesis was that the more quality control people there were inspecting, the higher the percentage of ware rejected. They found this to be supported and immediately issued an edict which cut the quality control group in half. Not only was the group reduced in size, but the technique of inspecting was adjusted so that there would be less interference with people on the floor. The new technique shifted to random sampling of lots after a series of manufacturing stages had been completed. During this period quality control got a new supervisor, Dick Main. Main, like Brown, was a young Boise up and comer. With Main came the notion of quality control engineering. More than only rejecting ware, his department was to assist both manufacturing and engineering in making the pieces good.

While the absolute number of the engineering department increased during the months preceding April 1970 with the inclusion of quality control, the number of men doing engineering work decreased from fifteen to fourteen and quality control itself decreased from twenty-three to twelve. With their new charter and heightened responsibility, the engineering group was required to enter into new and higher-quality relationships internally and with the rest of the plant. As observed, the common opinion of engineering was low, and the engineers' status was

*23*

next to nothing. In order for them to perform effectively, these conditions would have to change; making new machines and improving old ones would require the support and cooperation of the maintenance and manufacturing areas. Limited resources in engineering and limited resources on the floor, combined with the time constraints, all pointed to a necessary improvement in the relations of engineering with the rest of Becket.

MANUFACTURING: The manufacturing department was by far the largest of the departments at Becket, with twenty-eight monthly employees, and the most influential. With its size, uncontroverted status, and history of good economy, the manufacturing area was slow to respond to changing environmental demands. As Ben Morse, a department head, noted: "the times were too good . . . we [manufacturing] became fat, lazy, and content." With the declining economy, the new five-year plan, and Freeman's desire for efficiency, many changes were made in the manufacturing area and in manufacturing's relations with the rest of Becket.

One of the immediate consequences of Freeman's arrival was a break in the special connection the manufacturing men, especially the department heads, had with the plant manager. No longer would the manager meet with the manufacturing men and grant special considerations to them. Bob Smith, the production supervisor, was given the authority and responsibility to run the department as he saw fit. Freeman wanted no continuing influence on the floor. As if to emphasize this point, the production superintendent's office was moved away from Freeman's office, thus giving Smith the opportunity to "finally become his own man . . . it permitted Bob to bloom. . . ." It was also quickly established that manufacturing would have to assume a new position relative to both engineering and staff. While manufacturing remained the most important area at Becket, Freeman made it clear that manufacturing was "not to be the whole world" and that it would have to adjust to a relatively lower position of influence. While it was established that manufacturing was not as influential as before, there could be no doubt of its being the leading system in the plant. In fact, Smith was seen as the plant manager whenever Freeman was away and ran the plant on a day-to-day basis for all but the most difficult problems.

With the realigned power distribution affecting the manufacturing area, there were other structural changes to be contended with. Before Freeman, the manufacturing area can be described best by Chart 1.

The area was differentiated into two levels and each level was very wide. Six departmental heads and maintenance reported to Smith. Each

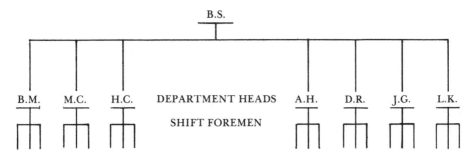

*Chart 1: Manufacturing Department, January 1970*

department head had responsibility for one phase of the manufacturing process and had two to three shift foremen reporting solely to him. With this large size went coordination problems. The technical interdependence between the groups was high; yet, the degree of cooperation and problem-solving ability was low. Intergroup relationships were hampered primarily by the myopic viewpoints of the department heads. Each man considered his own area and the attitudes were generally "to hell with the other guy's problems." Also of a low quality were the intragroup relationships. Often the shift foremen noted that they saw themselves as only figureheads, cut off from the information and influence lines. Little information or job authority was given to most of the shift foremen. Much of the foremen's work was done by the department head or he was directly supervised from decision to decision. These perceptions were shared by others throughout the plant and this too affected the shift foreman's ability to do his job. This effect was particularly highlighted in their dealings with the union. The manufacturing structure was so fat that each department had little responsibility. The amount of responsibility was reduced even further by the time it reached the shift foremen. In essence, both the shift foremen and the department head had similar time perspectives and thus overlapping activities. The problem was not in the number of levels of authority, but in the number of men at each level, the finite amount of work to be done, and the short time perspective throughout the plant.

These structural problems, combined with the fact that the twenty-eight monthly employees could not be justified under Freeman's accounting system, pointed to a need for change. Changes in the manufacturing area, however, had to be made with respect to unique conditions in the department itself. The monthly people had a mean service of twenty years, and by Boise tradition men with that service length cannot be dismissed for efficiency reasons. Although Freeman and Smith did not have a free hand in cutting the size of the department, they did initiate an informal retirement program for the senior men. No senior men were forced to retire; yet, the "advantages of retiring early" and the older men's marginality were stressed. These constraints considered, the changes shown in Chart 2 had been made by April 1970:

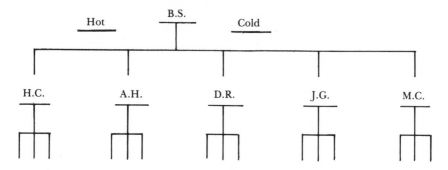

*Chart 2: Manufacturing Department, April 1970*

By April, two department heads and six shift foremen positions had been eliminated. These cuts in personnel were the first that were to occur in the manufacturing area over the next year. The structure was trimmed so that gradually two informal groups, the hot and cold ends of the plant, arose naturally. Because of the technology and the physical layout of the floor H.C. and A.H. had to work together on the hot end, while D.R. and J.G. worked together on the cold side. Within the two ends, the intergroup relationships improved since the increased level of responsibility could only be carried out with close cooperation between the two department heads, especially since the department heads took on the extra responsibility without distributing more decision-making power to their shift foremen. The reduction from three to two department heads in each area also reduced the potential for interarea coalitions. Inappropriate competition between the two ends, that is between H.C. and A.H. against D.R. and J.G., remained. The amount of contact and cooperation between ends remained less than required for maximal meshing of the total manufacturing process. While intraend relations improved to some extent, the relationships between shift foremen and their department heads remained as poor as before (H.C. being the only exception). The changes in numbers did not have any real effect on the shift foremen's authority or responsibility. The poor relations were reflected in chaotic, confused, and strained intragroup relationships. While the department heads did have greater responsibility they did not distribute it to their shift foremen. With these changes in size, Smith and Freeman also pushed for changes in manufacturing relations with other departments. It must be recalled that communications between the departments were best described as win-lose, with manufacturing used to winning. More direct contact between the departments and more contact at lower levels was encouraged with both engineering and staff.

Engineering and manufacturing had over the years established poor working relations. To combat this problem and to reinforce the newly constituted engineering group, Ben Morse, previously a well-respected manufacturing department head, was made project engineer. Morse reported to Brown and acted as an interface between the two areas. "Ben provides the engineers with the glass know-how. . . . Then they have ideas which he tempers and then sees to it that manufacturing listens . . . ." Besides having Morse to act as an integrator between the groups, Brown, Smith, and Freeman encouraged their men to work together to solve their problems at the level required. If a shift foreman had a problem with engineering, he was directed to take it up with the specific engineer involved, and the department heads were to be consulted only if the problem could not be solved at the lower levels. The problems between maintenance and engineering were attacked in the same manner. The active support of Freeman for engineering helped overcome the built-up manufacturing dislike for engineering.

The communication and cooperation problems between manufacturing and staff were different from the problems between manufacturing and engineering. Where engineering and manufacturing had to work together on specific problems, staff and manufacturing had to communicate accurate information between the two areas. Because of the history of manufacturing domination, simple two-way communications were difficult, a problem which was exacerbated when the expediters were eliminated as linking people between the two areas. At the production-staff interface the technique of using greater interaction and lower-level problem solving was also encouraged with little success.

The new emphasis in the manufacturing area was on the necessity for teamwork and an end to the nearsighted concern with one department or area. A wider perspective was established as a prerequisite for success at the individual, group, and area levels. This wider perspective involved a change in the goals and time orientation for each level of the hierarchy and a consequent change in the relationships throughout the plant. No longer was success defined solely by the amount of glass out the door, but now it included problem-solving ability within and without one's own area.

The changed authority distribution, the increased importance assigned to engineering, the "tight ship" philosophy practiced by Freeman and his team contributed to the cultural change at Becket. Of special importance to the manufacturing area was insecurity arising from both the overall pruning of the manufacturing area and the potential technological changes with engineering improvements. Also, of special concern was its lowered plant influence overall. Where other groups at Becket had to respond to an increase in influence, it was manufacturing that had to react to others' gains and had to adjust to its loss in control.

STAFF: An apt summary description of the staff group at Becket was provided by an interviewee: "Planning merely worked for manufacturing . . .and as such tended to fly by the seats of their pants . . . ." Their style was management by crisis while their time perspective coincided with manufacturing's short-time, long-run view of the world. In context with the changes described above and in line with Freeman's push for improvements at Becket, changes in the staff area were not a surprise.

The most siginficant change initiated by Freeman and his team was the emancipation of the staff group from manufacturing's control. A direct consequence of taking away some of manufacturing's influence was the increase in the influence of the staff area. The void made by taking decision-making power from manufacturing was filled with the enhanced mandate of the staff area. With this new freedom from the day-to-day view of production, both purchasing and scheduling could take a longer-range perspective. Given the five-year and yearly goals, it was staff's new mandate to see to it that the goals were pursued and reached on a period-by-period basis. With this new arrangement, staff made weekly and period commitments (a period being equal to four weeks) with respect to yearly plans and knowledge of the needs and capabilities of the manufacturing area. This sequencing was a reverse of the influence before April 1970. Planning established the schedules that manufacturing had to meet, and purchasing had to make sure that the right materials were available. The special-order category (20 percent of Becket's volume) was handled in a crisis fashion since these items could not be planned in advance; yet, here too the sequencing of influence was shifted from manufacturing to planning.

To aid in this change and to promote a more effective staff function there were two further changes. Most immediately visible was the elimination of the six expediters. Previously, the expediters had interfaced between manufacturing and staff and had kept track of work progress, inventory counts, and material supply. Eventually, they had become distinctly manufacturing oriented. Rather than acting as an interface between the two areas, the expediters were really the only direct contact staff had with manufacturing. Their elimination forced direct contact between the two areas. As was observed: "No longer could the expediters be used as a crutch between the groups . . . ."

The other change was in the use of the computer. Initially installed by Mitchell in April 1968, the computer was directed to the problems of scheduling, inventory control, and production mix. The goal was to reduce scheduling, purchasing, and stock errors by systematizing as much of the staff function as possible. While the phase-in process was recognized as a long-term project, the intentions were clear, to make more efficient the newly reversed order of influence between staff and manufacturing.

This new goal required that new relationships be established with both manufacturing and engineering. Most importantly, trust, improved communications, and some problem-solving ability had to be established with production. If problems arose in either area, quick and accurate feedback would be necessary to keep the production cycle as smooth and efficient as possible. This relationship was especially problematical and, as will be seen later on, was a constant weak spot in the Becket work process. The staff relation with engineering had to be initiated since engineering applications had to be properly phased in by members of the staff.

As was true with the manufacturing group, the staff area was deemed fat by Freeman and it too took a personnel loss. From a group consisting of six supervisors and sixteen weekly people; the staff area was cut to four monthly and seven weekly people (see pp. 39-43 for details). Yet unlike manufacturing, the staff group had increased responsibility above and beyond that expected with the decrease in personnel. By April 1970 the staff area had 25 percent fewer people on the job, a new set of objectives, a new process for doing the job; and an underused computer; and staff faced great pressure to get the job done well.

FREEMAN AND THE TOP TEAM: Throughout the work above, March 1970 has been used as a base line. This date was chosen because it was the time that Freeman arrived at Becket. It is tempting to credit Freeman with Becket's changes; yet, it cannot be that simple. The real credit for change must go to Freeman and his team, for it was this team that carried the spirit of change, innovation, and risk taking throughout the plant. Freeman was the stimulus and a constant pusher for newness; yet, it was his team that actually diffused this spirit through the plant. April 1970 will be used as a base line because it marks the formal emergence of Freeman's team at Becket.

Freeman's team consisted of Brooks, Brown, Smith, O'Connor, Winters, and McCall. The average age was thirty-two, compared to the Becket mean of forty-five. Of the seven members, five were either new to Becket or in a new position. Early in Freeman's stay, the group met out of the plant over a period of weeks to discuss Becket's condition and to develop goals, objectives, and methods to reach those goals. Basically their desire was to make Becket more dynamic and competitive and to "pull the plant out of its fixation with the status quo." (See the discussion of five-year and yearly plans on p. 21.) Freeman redefined the role of plant manager and production superintendent. Mitchell had been intimately concerned with day-to-day affairs to the exclusion of the production superintendent; Freeman changed this. While overall daily running of the plant was given to Smith, Freeman was to be concerned with Becket's environment and his time perspective would be in the six-month to five-year range. In short, Freeman was to look outward and Smith to look inward and take care of the plant on a day-to-day basis.

Freeman himself was seen as a pusher, a driver for change and increased effectiveness. His criteria for success were simple and direct and his actions showed him to be honest and consistent in application. He felt that if a person could not monetarily justify his existence at Becket, he should not be working at the plant. Freeman's desire and his push for efficiency was quickly picked up by his young, eager-to-please team. Here it might be well to reemphasize the cultural power available to Freeman. His team was made up of young men with real ambitions to move in Boise. At Boise, mobility and career aspects of one's job are an especially important factor of the boss-subordinate relationship, and Freeman's star made this an especially important factor not only with his team, but with all the monthly employees in the plant. Freeman was realistically seen as a good man to perform for. Ideas held strongly by Freeman thus received a higher commitment than was typical. This effect was also strong at the other end of the spectrum. Among the older manufacturing men there was a desire to be of help in promoting Freeman to further heights at Boise. As one older manufacturing man said: "I'd like to help a future vice president . . . ."

Besides this change in culture or philosophy which Freeman typified, he also changed the plant manager's relationships with other managers at Becket. No one group or department had special influence with the new man. With the equalization of influence, Freeman emphasized the team nature of his top staff. Few decisions were made by him directly, and more of Becket's decisions were shaped by his team. Freeman emphasized honest, open communications and the importance of feedback and combined this emphasis with a democratic style of directing his team.

Freeman and his team made a conscious effort to shape a definite managerial philosophy at Becket where before there had been no consistency. The change was from very loose crisis-by-crisis management to more ambitious management by participation in goal and objective setting within the constraints of the five-year and yearly plans. Once the goals were set, each manager was given a free hand to accomplish these goals as he saw fit. Thus, a basic shift in managerial style, one towards more openness, candor, problem solving, problem facing, and ambition, was encouraged and practiced by the most influential men at Becket.

A new ideology developed at Becket, a new culture personified by the plant manager and his team. It was an ideology of change, of taking more responsibility, of teamwork to push Becket to a more respectable budget position even if orders were declining. This ideology of change and the push for change, however, came as a great shock to many monthly employees at Becket. Their perceptions of this new managerial philosophy was one of uncertainty, soon to become simple insecurity. Expectations, goals, evaluation procedures were rapidly changed by this new spirit. A declining economy with the resultant lack of job possibilities, complete with the push for performance and the rapid changes, all led to an easy description of Becket personnel, insecure and up-tight. The further changes and the consequent response of Becket personnel must be seen in the light of this new culture.

## APRIL 1970 TO MARCH 1971

The economic picture facing the plant during this period showed no improvement. The drop in orders that started in 1968 continued unabated through 1970 and into the first half of 1971. During this time total sales dollars did not increase at all, the plant volume figures for 1970 showed a small decrease over 1969, and the productivity figure increased by only 1.8 percent. During the year both the hourly and monthly levels were cut in personnel. Hourly level was down to 333 employees and the monthly to thirty-five, a cut of twenty. The plant total was down to 409 by the end of the year. Thus, the economic conditions that greeted Freeman upon his arrival at Becket did not let up and the pressure from corporate headquarters was to keep all plants running at least at budget levels. Overall plant manning levels dropped sharply and productivity increased incrementally.

ENGINEERING: The engineering group at Becket encountered a radically new approach to life with the arrival of Brown and Freeman. It was given a new mandate and the importance of its work for the future of Becket was emphasized. Most affecting the men in the department were these factors: the shift in emphasis to the project concept from fire

*31*

fighting, new evaluation criteria, a large increase in the amount of work expected and the resultant pressure to perform, and the expectations and professional career emphasis of Brown.

As a result of a number of policy- and goal-setting meetings held in May, each engineering group set up projects and project goals. With these projects agreed upon, each area set to its task. Whether project dates were met or not, and they usually were not, over the year the projects did get completed, and Becket for the first time in many years began to improve its processes and techniques. Even with the poor cooperation and strained relationships with both maintenance and manufacturing, the fact is that engineering changes did occur at Becket during 1970. For the first time a totally on-line automated process was well on its way to completion. Plans for greater emphasis on automated processes in other parts of the plant were also being worked upon. Examples of completed projects by March 1971 include a remodeled swanson machine, silk-screen process improvements, and a new vial process.

While the direct results of the projects were many, the combination of the 100 percent evaluation criterion, the increase in the amount of work desired, and the constant pull of firefighting demands led to very consistent attitudes in the engineering department. The people were insecure, aggravated, and frustrated with the new engineering demands. Comments of "sweat shop," "slave camp," and "the total lack of considera-tion ... even the hourlies are treated better ..." were typical. The engineers were in a classic bind. On the one hand they were evaluated as to the quality and punctuality of their projects, but on the other hand they were expected and required to keep the manufacturing floor running smoothly on a day-to-day basis. The 20 percent firefighting figure issued by Brown was often exceeded, leaving the engineers with much less free time for their projects. The results of these conditions coupled with the hard evaluation procedures were pervasive insecurity and exacerbated tension in the department. This effect was heightened in the case of the middle-aged engineer whose marketability was poor and who was young enough to fear being laid off. As the year wore on and the projects came due, the pressure and tension increased. With this increase in pressure, departmental norms were such that fifty to sixty hours a week, including at least one day during the weekend, were standard. During this period the departmental relationships at meetings and informally indicated good working relations between levels. While tensions were high, the adversity seemed to bring the engineers together. The feelings toward Brown, though, were mixed. While some men believed that he pushed too hard, most felt that the pressure originated independently of Brown. Further, he worked as long and as hard as his men and made group decisions whenever possible. Some men felt that Brown used insecurity as a threat; yet, they never verbalized this feeling to him.

Brown's perspective on his area was very different. He recognized the situation, yet felt that it was healthy. He believed that a top flight engineering group must work in a cycle: from ambitious goals to risky projects to pressure and hard work to project completion and "finally to a big drunk." He believed that once his department got their projects completed that the men "would look back and be proud" and that he would then have the best engineering group in the Boise Company. At the same time, however, he noted that the men could not take this pressure for too much longer without a break.

The changes in culture in the engineering area necessitated changes in relations within and without the department. Within the department itself the effects were obvious. The pace of the room, the drawn and tired look on most of the engineer's faces by four o'clck underlined the tension. To meet the increased requirements, internal organizing was required especially for scheduling maintenance times for projects. While competition for scarce resources (time, materials) was vigorous, intradepartmental coordination and process problems were worked out for the most part collaboratively. For instance task groups were established to allot scarce maintenance time, and weekly meetings were held to review past problems and to organize for the next week. Meetings in the engineering area were typically characterized by full participation, openness, and a desire to confront problems and get them solved as effectively as possible. Brown ran his meeting in a very open fashion. Of the meetings the author attended, Brown only once made a unilateral decision (under crisis); the rest were made in a participative fashion. In all, while the pressure increased dramatically, the department pulled together internally to make the most of its resources.

Included in the engineering area was the quality control group. Although this group did not directly interact with the engineers, they must be included in this engineering section because the rest of the plant considered them to be engineering. As mentioned before, the quality control group was cut in half and found itself with a new supervisor, Dick Main, after Freeman's arrival. During the year Main initiated a new quality control concept called quality engineering. This concept emphasized not only the necessity of rejecting glassware, but also a responsibility to get it repaired. The basic quality control change was in physical inspection procedures. With the cut in personnel the inspectors randomly checked the glassware at only a few critical areas on the manufacturing floor rather than at each station as before. Then, if a lot was rejected, quality control was to work with manufacturing and engineering to improve the defect. Also, quality control was to cooperate with engineering and manufacturing to standardize glass specifications and to improve the overall quality of the Becket glassware. These new tasks entailed developing new relationships throughout the plant and overcoming stigmas handed down over the years.

The emphasis on new projects and processes in engineering required the cooperation and assistance of the maintenance, staff, and manufacturing groups. Here it must be remembered that the history and place of engineering at Becket worked against quality collaboration especially with maintenance and manufacturing. Manufacturing's cooperation was needed to help in effective machine-process design and to keep the brush fire demands as low as possible. Maintenance's assistance and cooperation was required in prototype design, for suggestions in machine and tool needs, and for providing feedback in installing new systems. Staff's support was also required, although in a more secondary way, to keep the jobs and materials in step with engineering modifications. All these new relationships had to be established for the engineering group to better its effectiveness. To develop those relations, however, took time and patience, which was just what the engineers did not have. As a result the working cooperation received by the majority of the engineers was very poor and the rate of improvement was incremental if there was any. There were individual differences; yet, for the most part problem-solving ability was of a low quality (in terms of solution stability or effectiveness) between engineering and other departments. There was very little contact with the shift foremen except during crises on the floor. During these stress-filled occasions, friendships did not thrive. Ben Morse was a notable exception as "he was able to get help anywhere in the plant . . . . " He worked very hard as an integrator and did all he could to reconcile manufacturing and the engineering group. In his words he was a "cheerleader . . . or handholder for both areas . . . . " Morse was the only engineer to have frequent contact with manufacturing and was the only engineer able to work effectively on the floor. He did much to shift the opinion of the engineering people; yet, as he noted, "it was a long and slow process at best."

In summary, by March 1971 the engineering department at Becket was radically transformed. Although engineering did contribute new projects and processes to the plant and did "contribute to the Becket till," the contributions also yielded some real dysfunctional consequences. Insecurity and tension ran high in the group, with each engineer operating under the perceived reality that, if his project was not done on schedule and if fires were not kept to a minimum, there was a real possibility that he might be out of a job. While projects did get completed, they were often done with very poor relations with other departments at Becket. Intradepartmental relationships were good, while the interdepartmental relations below the manager level remained poor and a cause of extra difficulties for the engineers.

MANUFACTURING: April 1970 to March 1971 was a period of constant adjustment for the manufacturing department. Their power and numbers had been severely jolted. The changes mentioned in the last section and other changes initiated throughout the year began to have an effect. Unlike the engineering or staff groups, manufacturing did not increase in influence, status, or total work load during the year. In fact, all of these factors decreased along with the number of men in the area. The loss in status and power produced a kind of withdrawal of the manufacturing men from the other functional areas into themselves and toward Smith as their "new" production superintendent. The author's interviews and observations were consistent: the factor that most affected the manufacturing men was the dramatic loss in personnel. Insecurity followed naturally.

The year was marked with many cuts in the number of hourly employees on the floor including a layoff of thirty-three workers in March, the largest layoff in Becket's history. In addition to the decrease in the number of people on the floor came decreases in the number of shift foremen and the consequent increased responsibility for the remaining monthly employees. Eight shift foremen were let go or retired and no new people were brought in to fill the vacancies. As people were let go, jobs were combined and consolidated. There was no increase in the overall amount of work, but since there were fewer men available the work load increased at both the monthly and weekly levels. As in the engineering department, insecurity became prominent on the manufacturing floor; yet, in manufacturing the source of insecurity was slightly different. It arose not so much out of evaluation apprehension, although that was a factor, as out of a fear of one's job being discontinued or combined. This uncertainty was felt by both the hourly and the monthly employees including the department heads. As a shift foreman said, "The people at this level are real up-tight . . . they don't know whether they are coming or going." Another observed: "One does not have to be a genius to know that if thirty hourlies are laid off then there is less of a need for shift foremen." In all, under the ideology espoused and practiced by Freeman and his team, the year April 1970 to March 1971 saw the manufacturing department pruned thinner and thinner. With the continuing work, with fewer men there, the amount of responsibility increased absolutely, especially at the department-head level, and there was a concomitant increase in the overall level of insecurity on the whole manufacturing floor. This insecurity was especially observable at the shift-foreman level since the foreman's options were much fewer than a department head's and he had no seniority rights as did the hourly workers.

With the cut in department heads to four, the manufacturing floor can be realistically conceptualized as two distinct yet mutually interdependent areas, the hot and cold ends. While there were individual differences between the department heads and the conditions of their areas, the relations between the areas are similar enough to allow for general statements about the manufacturing area as a whole. The intragroup relationships improved in the year being discussed. For example, within the finishing area, with the increase in responsibility and the inherent process interdependence the men worked together more collaboratively and mutually. The frequency of intradepartment shift-foremen interactions increased during the year as shift foremen within each department kept in constant contact to keep their areas in phase, but the relations of shift foremen with their department heads or manufacturing superintendent remained as poor as before. While there was much talk of pushing the decision making down and giving shift foremen more of a say in day-to-day activities, in all but a few cases this never happened. There was no perceived increase in authority delegated by the department heads to the shift foremen. Further, while shift foremen were encouraged by Smith and Freeman to become more involved and aware of plant action, they were not plugged into the flow of information. From the viewpoint of the shift foremen, information and authority stopped at the department-head level. These conditions were especially true in the cold end of the plant. In general, the common cry of the shift foremen was for more authority, responsibility, and information, "for actions to go along with the words."

This lack of information and participation was a source of frustration to the shift foremen and contributed to their intragroup fixation. Cooperation and mutual coordination between shift foremen of other departments was strained and infrequent. Rarely during work hours would a shift foreman be seen out of his area, and during common meetings the division around the tables was often by departmental areas. The attitude expressed was "let them [other departments] take care of their own problems, I'll take care of mine." Considering the necessary interdependence of the areas, this attitude caused inefficiency. The relations between the department heads was a reflection of the relations between the shift foremen (or was it vice versa?). The department heads in the hot end worked together well; yet, they did not work as well with the opposite end. As a department head observed: "to work best, both ends of the plant

year four of the six monthly people
ding the new manager, Bob Mazur.
D.W., were new to Becket altogether.
, consisting of B.M., M.M., L.S., D.W.,
n 1970 with the promotion of Mazur.
f the staff area was transformed from
n, fixed patterns of behavior, and
ion, and a desire to perform well. The
-two and each had at least one college

e in 1970, the department rapidly took
up was determined to start afresh with
ng. Being new in personnel, structure,
nally unencumbered by the relation-
verned the older group; but they did
relations with the other areas. Mazur
s group. Intradepartmental coopera-
antly emphasized and carried out by
nd informally every day, coffee breaks
unch hour would often find a staff area
given full responsibility for scheduling
ty for purchasing. Previously, the staff
sponsibility for both those functions.
and the mandate to improve its fit and
th Freeman, redefined his position to
both his area and Becket in general.
were unanimous and typified by the
est boss I have ever worked for . . . I
to prove myself now . . . ." Because the
problem so characteristic of the rest of
ey all knew that they had to perform,
Whether because they were new to the
, evaluation apprehension was never
the researcher in their dealings in the

st obvious and far-reaching change was
ff and manufacturing. With its new
n to plan, forecast, purchase, supply,
e best plan to meet budget and goals.
ncertainty of the environment and to
e plant in general with information and
ole, the technology of the plant was

must be in constant contact, like two gears. In the past we have been more
uncoupled than not . . . . " The men in the two areas associated with each
other differentially at meetings and during the lunch breaks. The pattern
of interactions within and between the areas can best be summarized with
a chart:

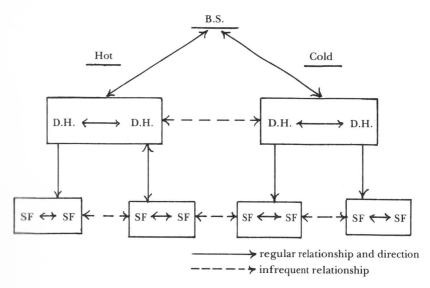

*Chart 3: Patterns of Interactions in the Manufacturing Department,*
*April 1970 – March 1971*

As can be seen, there were individual differences in both areas, but
overall horizontal, vertical, and diagonal lines of communication were
limited and many were only one way. It is obvious, then, why during this
period many problems were acted upon with missing or incomplete
information. Information was in the system yet not completely available.
It must be added that this is a description of the steady-state conditions in
the areas. When things were going well interactions increased; when
crises arose the reverse was true. In all, the year to March 1971 found the
relationships in the manufacturing area somewhat different. While
interactions were of a generally higher frequency and quality within level
and within area (for example, shift foremen in the grinding area or
department heads in the hot end), most other horizontal, vertical, and
diagonal relationships remained poor and infrequent. Most boss and
subordinate relations remained unilateral.

The changes during the year did not have any positive effect on the
patterns of interactions between functional departments, except at the

manager level. The lowering of manufacturing status and the relative increase in status to both staff and engineering, combined with the pervasive insecurity, were not easy to adjust to.

The relation of both manufacturing and maintenance to engineering remained full of conflict. The engineers had great difficulty in overcoming the disrespect and general mistrust of the men on the floor. To make matters worse, the engineers were as a group, significantly younger and more educated than the manufacturing men. There was much hostility on the floor: "Those young punks . . . they don't know what glass is really all about . . ." or "they've been to college . . . yet I've worked here for years and it's experience that really counts . . . . " Even though engineering projects were supported by Smith and Freeman, the men on the floor saw engineering as time away from their real jobs, a secondary consideration. Considering the other primary pressures on the manufacturing men, the engineering and manufacturing relationship was strained at best. Their goals, time perspective, evaluation criteria and overall organizational perspective were basically at odds. The situation with the maintenance area was very similar. The two areas had to work together on design, layout, and installation of new machines and systems; yet, they communicated very poorly with each other. Maintenance would be insulted because they often were not consulted on process design and on layout problems, while the engineers resented maintenance's simplistic view of engineering and their resistance to new and innovative ideas. The relationship between the two groups was strained at best and hostile at worst as can be seen by this quote: "I wanted to throw that blasted young engineer into the machine."

The patterns of interactions between the staff area and manufacturing changed of necessity. Under the new structure, the staff group made up schedules and purchased the materials with respect to overall plant goals. This system required constant feedback and information flow between the two areas, especially with the large volume of special orders. Accurate information flow was especially important as the period wore on since scheduling would often make changes, based on manufacturing feedback, to accommodate specials that would increase receipts. The primary vehicles to accomplish these communication and cooperation needs were biweekly planning meetings. At these meetings the staff groups would alert the manufacturing department heads to the current plant figures with respect to the goals; manufacturing also provided information on the state of the floor. Each scheduled item was discussed and much emphasis was given to special orders (these meetings will be described in greater detail on pp. 41-42). The planning meetings were very poor by any standard. They, in fact, reflected the basic problem between the two

completely remanned. During the
were new to their positions, inclu
Three of the men, B.B., B.R., and
The development of the new group
B.B., and B.R., was completed late
With this switch, the monthly level
one of relative shortness of visi
advanced age to one of youth, ambi
average age of the group was thirty
degree.

With the promotion of Mazur lat
on its new image and role. The gro
both manufacturing and engineeri
and mandate, the group was inte
ships, customs, and norms that go
have to work in establishing new
emphasized the team nature of hi
tion and collaboration were const
Mazur. The group met formally a
were often held together, and the l
bridge game in progress. L.S. was
and B.B. was given full responsibil
manager had taken day-to-day re
B.R. was given the systems position
performance at Becket. Mazur, w
include longer-range planning fo
The reactions of the new staff
following comment: "Bob is the b
really feel that I'm getting a chance
staff group was so new, the security
the plant was absent. Although th
there was no fear of jobs being cut
positions or because of their yout
mentioned by staff or observed b
plant.

Outside of the staff area, the mo
the new relationship between st
mandate, it was the staff's functi
and, in general, keep Becket on t
The group was to mediate the u
supply both manufacturing and th
direction. To help in this new

improved. In 1968 an IBM 360 computer was brought to Becket. It was during the year 1970 to 1971 that the machine began to reach its potential and to pay its way. Although there were many problems in phasing the machine in, the computer was used in scheduling, purchasing, and accounting.

With the elimination of the expediters and the formal separation in powers between staff and manufacturing, it is not surprising to find that the greatest intergroup change experienced by staff was with the manufacturing area. Staff was required to transfer information in the form of schedules, goals, and stock assurances to the manufacturing men. Further, the goals had to be made up with manufacturing capabilities, capacity, and situations in mind. This required two-way communications. Only with collaboration and effective problem solving could the staff work to its potential.

The main vehicle for information transfer, in both directions, was a biweekly planning meeting. The department heads, the production superintendent, and the monthly staff attended the meetings. The meetings were chaired by Smith and were always the same. From week to week the physical layout of the meeting was constant. The manufacturing men sat at one end of the table close to Smith, with the hot shift foremen and department heads on one side of him and the cold on the other. The staff men either sat outside of the main table or at the other end. Others attending, engineers for instance, sat between the two ends. There was first a general information session in which each man had a chance to let people know what important events were happening in his area. This part of the meeting was attended by the engineering department heads. Most people passed; often the only responses came after a question from Smith. This communication part of the meeting was always completed in less than five minutes. Next, Mike McCall, the comptroller, reviewed the overall plant figures. He stressed the important plant indicators and compared them to goals for the period. Again, very few questions were asked except by either Mazur or Smith. At this point the engineers left and the planning session began. For the next hour, Len Samules, the scheduler, discussed the period commitments and detailed each stock area with respect to forecast, budget, and present position. The purpose was to keep the manufacturing men abreast of the period numbers so that an effective schedule could be established for the rest of the period. Questions and comments were encouraged by Smith but he was usually the only one to make them. The manufacturing men responded only when their particular area was threatened by a shortage in glassware, short runs, or the like. These bursts of chatter were win or lose, sarcastic, or accusing in nature. Most of the action was nonverbal or subaudible as

*41*

the manufacturing men would often respond with upset faces, frowns, or quiet discussions among themselves. They tended to slouch in their chairs and, in all, gave the impression of being very bored and uncomfortable. The degree of involvement at the meetings was low and virtually all the decisions were made by Smith, the scheduler, or Mazur.

This description of a planning meeting should highlight a basic problem at Becket over the year in question: staff and production communication and trust. Staff was young and educated, while manufacturing was older and experienced. Staff was eager "to do big things" and to innovate, while manufacturing was less mobility conscious and more prone to protect the status quo. It follows that there was constant tension between the department heads and the men who made the budgets. A typical source of conflict was the run length of an item. Manufacturing enjoyed the long runs, while staff often wanted to break up runs for inventory or scheduling reasons. There was also the problem between the two areas in understanding of terminology. Often people in manufacturing would misinterpret McCall or Samules or vice versa. There was little effort to correct this problem or to recognize it as a problem, although it was common knowledge that most of the manufacturing men did not have a way with numbers. Thus, the relationship between staff and manufacturing was characterized by mistrust and poor collaboration. Whatever its causes, mistrust remained a constant source of conflict and inefficiency throughout the year. To make the situation worse, it must be remembered that the shift foremen rarely left their areas and rarely talked directly with the staff. The information in and to their areas was filtered through the department heads before it got to staff. This process was both slow and not free from distortion. For instance, Mazur called a shift foreman who was to pack a special item by closing. Mazur had talked to the department head in the morning about the special; yet, the message had not reached the foreman by three thirty. As a result of the poor communication between the areas many brush fires, such as a lack of glassware, overproduction, or an imbalance in hourly workers on certain jobs, erupted on the floor. These smaller fires were fanned by poor information flow, and at times small problems rose to major proportions requiring Smith or Freeman to be called in.

The staff relation with the engineering group was much less complex because there was significantly less need to interact with each other; yet, the problems were there. They were of a different kind from those with manufacturing and were of a small dollar and time magnitude. The changes in the relationships between the two areas arose with changes in processes, machines, or techniques. Each engineering change that affected the manufacturing floor also directly affected the staff. For instance, scheduling a new process would have to be updated along with a potential change in materials needed. Changes made by the engineers had to be coordinated with both the manufacturing and staff schedules. Although rescheduling had always been a function of the staff, none had been done in recent Becket times because of the engineers' history. Problems arose in the bookkeeping, and the "trailer system" that accompanied each engineering change fell behind over the year. The problem was getting the two groups together to iron out the differences and to fill in the information gaps and it was not addressed until Mazur arrived as the new manager. In all, the basic problem between staff and engineering involved role confusion and the inevitable problems that arise when groups take on new and expanded responsibilities. Their problem was qualitatively and quantitatively different from the tense, conflict-ridden relationships characteristic of staff and manufacturing.

The April 1970 to March 1971 year was one full of changes for the staff area. The makeup of the group changed both in size and character. The task and mandate were also expanded and more formally defined, and the technology of the group was continually being improved. The staff relations with other groups ranged from confused and intermittent with engineering to mistrustful and uncollaborative with manufacturing.

FREEMAN AND THE TOP TEAM: The year April 1970 to March 1971 saw the influence of Freeman and his top team increase. By March 1971, Freeman's team consisted of Brown, Brooks, McCall, O'Connor, Smith, and Mazur. Four of the six men were new to their positions since the arrival of Freeman, and the oldest (Smith) was thirty-seven. As has been observed, the most critical position at Becket is plant manager. During the year, Freeman reinforced the initial impression he had made and reaffirmed that he was a "marked man in Boise's future."

"Doug had a perfect pedigree for Boise." As a result, he was not seen as a plant manager, but rather as a future vice president fulfilling the necessary prerequisites. This reality made his life as plant manager very different from what it would have been for any other man. For instance, the plant manager's relation with his boss was nonexistent. As was noted: "Dick Thompson [Freeman's boss] used a laissez faire type of supervision because he was afraid of pushing or directing Freeman . . . ." Freeman then was able to do with Becket as he wished as long as he met the basic requirements set for all plant managers. Given this fact, Freeman was able to plan more ambitiously and to take more risks than the typical manager. In the same vein, Freeman was able to get commitment and actual support from outside Becket on many projects that normally would have to be solved internally or not at all (for example, commitment from research park on a micropipette machine). Internally, he took advantage of his distinctiveness and during the year strove to make Becket into a "showcase for Boise." During the year Freeman was an agent of change at Becket. With his goals in mind, goals very similar to the top team's goals mentioned in the last section, Freeman set out to shape and develop Becket with his team. The year in discussion saw the first phase of this process.

As far as interpersonal relationships were concerned, Freeman's actions throughout the year reinforced initial impressions. Below the top team, Doug was seen as "quiet," "introspective," "aloof," and, by many, as just a "cold man." During the year he moved his office door away from the main corridor and placed his secretary between the corridor and his new entrance. People quickly got the impression that, unlike Mitchell, he did not enjoy socializing with the employees. The effect of his presence at meetings was immediate and obvious. Upon his entrance, usually unexpected, people would sit up quite straight and direct all attention to him. His questions were sharp and direct and, combined with his complete knowledge of the plant, his presence was uncomfortable for most. Meetings became quieter with people responding only when asked. Any meeting that Freeman attended became in reality a show for him, with real dialogue at a minimum in a heavy, noninvolving atmosphere. Although he was seen as completely task oriented, just about every interviewee commented at least once on how "Doug is the best man I have ever worked for . . . ." A consistent impression seemed to be that although he was a "hard-nosed pusher," he was always fair, honest, and direct. Nevertheless, although the people below the top team admitted that they respected Freeman, at the same time they did not speak to him openly or directly. "The answers he received were mostly the answers he wanted."

Freeman's relation with his top team was different in degree rather than in kind. The most obvious difference was the social relationships between members of the team and Doug. Their staff meetings were considerably more open and not totally task oriented; yet, the relationships among the top team members were different from their relationships with Freeman. It was often admitted that the kind of feedback that the plant manager received was quite different from and of a lower quality than that which occurred among the team members. His strongly held ideas often went unchallenged, although when he was undecided there was much activity in their meetings. In general, his team would shun direct conflict with him. Contacts between the plant manager and his team were typically initiated by Freeman. Each day he would walk through the plant and drop into their offices. The contact among the team members was of a higher frequency and more mutually initiated.

In summary, throughout the year Freeman established and reinforced his task-oriented style. He was perceived by men below the top team as cold, equivocal, and aloof. A "king effect" developed as a result of the cultural givens of the plant manager and of his own style and background.

The year also brought maturation and development of his top team. As was previously noted, it was the top team that actually carried the ideology of change, innovation, cooperation, and risk taking throughout the plant. Over and above this change philosophy, the team also espoused and practiced a definite brand of managerial style. Each team member (except Brown) had been through at least Phase One of Blake and Mouton's managerial grid program and as such tried to practice the 9,9 ideal.

As a team they met frequently, both in formal meetings and informally in each other's offices. With Freeman setting the style, the team set ambitions and goals for Becket. Once the goals were established, the team members carried them to their areas. Within each department the group set their own goals and criteria for success consistent with the overall goals. At the top-team level, the interdepartment conflict mentioned before took the form of role ambiguity and role conflict. These problems were always discussed and worked through in an open and participative manner. Yet, even if the managers confronted the conflicts, they well realized that their departments did not. Concern for interdepartmental conflict, the lack of problem-solving abilities, and the unwillingness to take a more systematic view of Becket were all reasons that the team used to justify their decision to commit Becket to a Blake and Mouton organizational development program. While the decision was the team's, it was initiated and actively supported by Freeman. Carl Hoffman of Boise's organization research and development group was called in as their consultant.

Over the year this group of managers became the dynamic force behind the evolution of Becket. Although the plant was beginning to pick up (for example, the 1.8 percent increase in productivity), the top team felt that "the work was being done the hard way." Their major problems were interdepartmental and intradepartmental, which were especially prominent in the manufacturing department. Insecurity of the lower managers contributed to the short-term perspective and particularly affected the members of Freeman's team. Mitchell had created a secure climate for his men and was himself socially oriented. Freeman's entrance suddenly cut this secure link, especially with the manufacturing men. The year found the top team forced to take on many socio-emotional problems based on the security issue, not to mention the potential performance decrements that went along with the insecurity. Their attitude seemed to be quite consistent with respect to the insecurity. "If a person is not doing his work he ought to be scared; if he is doing his job then he has nothing to worry about. . . . " was a typical comment. Their problem was convincing the men that they could do their jobs and that their jobs were in fact important.

The year found Freeman and the team concept more influential than they were in April 1970. The team espoused openness and candor along with tougher and riskier expectations and procedures for evaluation. An important observation made by the team during the year was that interdepartmental conflicts and the inability to communicate between and sometimes within departments had mutually reinforcing dysfunctional effects. The decision was made for a Blake and Mouton Phase One project to begin in April 1971.

## APRIL 1971 TO AUGUST 1971

To this point the story of Becket has been traced over thirty-seven months. While the plant did improve slightly in budget and productivity, the advances were made under complex plantwide stress. The last period was described quite vividly as "bloody and strained . . . . " Intervening variables (Likert, 1961) such as degree of mutual confidence and trust, quality of cooperation, work-group effectiveness, and conflict resolution techniques also were affected by the previous changes and all were of a low quality. This section covers the last period to be discussed and will describe the Phase One intervention which was aimed at these process-oriented variables. Throughout the period the whole managerial staff participated in the week-long program. This program, its effects on the men, and the consequent effects in the plant will be covered in this section.

Becket's economic environment continued to be hostile. The year 1971 brought no relief in the sales, order, or volume decline that began in 1968. Orders continued to decrease at a rate of approximately 4 percent per year, and the Boise economic forecast was for more of the same. In line with the decreasing volume was a continuation of layoffs among the hourly employees. With no let up in sight and Freeman's aggressiveness, the union activity increased during this period. Although the union situation will not be discussed, it was a continuing headache for management throughout the period. For example, because of seniority rules the layoff of thirty men in April required the reshuffling of another one hundred men with all the concomitant confusion and inefficiency. A second result of the decreases in the hourly work force was further decreases among the monthly employees, especially in manufacturing. In April the number of department heads on the manufacturing floor was decreased from four to two, while the number of shift foremen was decreased from fifteen to eight. One department head remained for each end of the plant and four shift foremen under each, in contrast to the three department heads in each area just eighteen months before. One of the displaced department heads was "promoted" to project engineer. His job was much like Morse's, to "coordinate and supervise the introduction of major [engineering] changes .... " This integrator position was created in response to the increased activity of engineering and the felt need for improved collaboration with manufacturing. The cuts were effected by a number of retirements and by a few organizational promotions. The top team was sensitive to the layoff or firing issue and made great efforts to let the remaining monthly employees know that they did not have to fear for their jobs. It was clear though that any vacated position would not be filled and that the extra responsibilities would be picked up by the remaining men. By early 1971 the monthly levels were thinned to the point that the job elimination aspect of insecurity was lessened. A common observation was "we've just gone too far with this pruning ... there is just too much responsibility to be effectively handled .... " As a consequence, the job-evaluation aspect of insecurity was increased because of the increased work loads and the high expectations. In all, the period from March to August 1971 saw a continued decline in orders and sales, a decrease in the hourly and monthly levels, greater union activity, continuing yet shifted insecurity, and a somewhat decreased level of structural change in terms of variables such as span of control or decision making. The major change during the period was aimed at the culture of the plant.

The period from March to July 1971 saw all the Becket monthly employees "go away to school." The program was introduced at a monthly meeting early in 1971 by Frank O'Connor (personnel manager) who was the "internal change agent." He described the program to the monthly employees as an educational experience that would help on the job and noted the need for increased communication between departments and with the hourly employees. He specifically tried to allay the evaluation apprehension initially evident and stressed the program's tool-related nature. He underplayed the academic nature of the Phase One seminar week. The other members of Freeman's team, most of whom had already been to a Phase One session, also discussed the benefits of the program in their areas. Hoffman was introduced and was available for questions and advice.

Phase One of the grid program is a week-long training session held away from the plant. Through a series of structured experiential learning episodes combined with lectures on interpersonal perception, conflict resolution, and the like, participants are exposed to the grid terminology, philosophy, and its ideal managerial type, 9,9. One of the advantages of the Blake and Mouton program is that it can be applied to an ongoing organization without major disruptions in operations. At Becket there were three separate grid schools set up so that on any one occasion there would be no more than eleven monthly employees out of the plant. (The Phase One sessions were not limited to men from Becket. The sessions included at least thirty other men from all over the Boise system representing all levels of management.) The first group went in mid-March. It included manufacturing and staff department heads, engineering group leaders, and a few shift foremen. The second group went in May and included engineers and shift foremen; the remainder of the Becket monthly employees went to school in July. The order of attendance at the three sessions was not random. The first session included men at the second level in the hierarchy so that when they returned they could do preliminary seeding work in their areas (Blake and Mouton, 1964). As each group returned from school their enthusiasm, excitement, and new knowledge of grid techniques were encouraged and reinforced by the top team. By the time the last group went to school they already knew much of the grid terminology, had seen its effects on their coworkers, and were less anxious than they had originally expected.

By July 1971 all Becket monthly workers had been to Phase One. These four months produced many observable changes in individual and group behavior. Whether these changes reflect stable internalized shifts in attitudes or are merely postexperience artifacts cannot be determined with the data on hand. Did the men learn new skills or were they merely unfrozen to use already existing skills? Maybe the men felt that they had survived the cuts in personnel and that management was investing in its remaining people. Perhaps the Phase One session was merely a cathartic experience in which they simply blew off some steam and remet each other in "camp conditions." These are each legitimate explanations. While these explanations cannot be refuted and probably are correct to a degree, the author feels that the primary benefit of the week away was the exposure to a simple yet different cognitive work framework and the resultant skills derivable from that framework (see Chapter Four for greater detail on the Phase One session). Whatever the reason, throughout the managerial level this was a period of dramatic behavioral changes. Both interview and observational data can be used to support this statement. Even using the researcher's tactics to remove demand characteristics (see Appendix Two), the interviews during this grid period were remarkably consistent. To a man, the opinion was that Phase One had been a very worthwhile week; a sample of comments include: "one of the best-spent weeks of my life . . . , " " . . . very healthy for the individuals involved and the organization . . . . " Perhaps an extreme reaction was this passage taken from an open letter to the Phase One director: "Except during my student time where we reached the same candor after maybe three years I have never experienced what happened last week! I have certainly not seen it in industry before. Thank you very much."

In addition to these positive remarks on the program, each man interviewed said that he had come from grid with new insights into himself, new ideas, and new ambitions for work. All perceived the week as personally meaningful and many noted that the grid lessons could be used to do one's job better. The tool aspect of the program was mentioned particularly frequently in the manufacturing areas. A systems perspective was also learned. Typical comments from the shift-foremen level and up were: "We must take an overall view of the plant," "as an organization we must realize the interdependence of the plant," and " . . . I now have a better feel for the problems in A's area . . . . " For instance, M.C. (maintenance) who before refused to cooperate with the engineers observed: "I am now able to give and take criticisms with the engineers without getting all upset . . . I no longer want to throw them to the machines as quickly . . . !" In all, there were two kinds of thoughts usually expressed in the postgrid interviews. One was a commitment to trying to change one's interpersonal style in a grid-oriented way towards more openness, confronting, and so on. The other was the opinion that employees had to take a more systematic point of view towards the plant operations.

While these interviews were exciting, they cannot be used as evidence for behavioral changes. Evidence to support interview data comes from observations. At the interpersonal level the researcher observed increased cooperation; increased openness; increased confronting; more problem solving at lower levels; increased spans of cognition; vocalized desire for more information and authority to go with increased responsibility; and a greater willingness to make commitments and take reasonable risks. These new kinds of behaviors were observed in the course of meetings, at informal gatherings, and at lunch gatherings. With the common grid experience new vocabulary and corresponding plant norms and values that rewarded grid-oriented behaviors developed rapidly. Examples of new kinds of behavior must include the increased mobility of the shift foremen outside of their departments and new group processes at meetings where openness was demanded, participation increased, and the decision-making level varied with the problem type.

During this period a greater number of problems were recognized and faced by people below the department-head level. As the men became more sensitized to the interdependence of the plant more problems were recognized. Contrary to expectations there was an increase in fires throughout the plant; yet, where before these had gone unnoticed until too late, during this period the tendency was to get together and work with the relevant people to "iron the many newfound problems out." It follows that there was an increase in the number of informal and spontaneous meetings and a general increase in plant mobility for the monthly work force. It was usual to observe small groups of men from different areas discussing a problem of common concern. Often groups of men would go out to dinner after a "friendly bet" on some plant problem was decided. In general, there was an increase in the number of meetings, a decrease in the number of men at any one meeting, and a general increase in the level of participation at these meetings. In addition to these obvious quantitative changes in the meetings there were also qualitative changes. The meetings were of a higher quality; seating arrangements were more random; more and different men initiated ideas; and there was more overt cooperation, trust, and mutual reinforcement. It was commented: "Our meetings tend to be freer floating . . . as compared to our old cat and dog matches . . . we are more open and honest . . . we now have constructive disagreements . . . . "

Phase One did have a real effect on the men in terms of what they said and how they acted. Of course, these changes were not completely internalized quickly, and the men always had their old styles to rely on. These relapses were especially evident in times of crisis or towards the end of a four-week period. Nevertheless, grid provided the men with a simple yet very different kind of cognitive framework which both fit well given the structure of the plant and, as importantly, was vigorously supported by Freeman and his top team.

With the interpersonal changes in mind, the interdepartmental and intramanufacturing changes follow. The April 1970 to March 1971 period concluded with the interdepartmental relations characterized as "mistrustful and uncollaborative," "confused and intermittent," or "generally resentful of being distracted." By August 1971 the above labels were already dated.

MANUFACTURING AND STAFF: Indicative of the change in these two areas was the change in the planning meeting. Early in April it was abolished. Its demise brings out many of the changes in the Becket culture in general and in staff and manufacturing in particular. After one Tuesday planning meeting, the manufacturing department met to critique the customary meeting (critiquing was learned at grid). They felt that transfer of information was the basic reason for the meeting, and as a group they decided that the setup of the planning meeting was poor from their point of view. A meeting was then called to discuss the situation with the staff people who, they found, were also dissatisfied with the meeting arrangement. They discussed the necessity of dispersing critical and accurate information and the needs of the separate departments and individuals involved and came up with an alternative to the "weekly planning farce." Since the manufacturing men had set up daily production meetings, it was decided to have the staff attend whenever they wanted. To take care of the regular information flow, the staff agreed to print up the weekly figures and distribute them to all monthly employees in the plant. With this setup the original function of the planning meeting was met; yet, instead of the two-hour weekly meeting, staff and manufacturing could meet on any day to discuss immediate problems, while plant figures were simply compiled and distributed to the men as needed.

The number of informal meetings, at all levels, between the two areas also increased. Shift foremen and schedulers or purchasers were often in each others' areas working directly together. While the number of fires increased, these tended to be worked out with the combination of new planning meetings, the informal contacts, and the increased interpersonal competence. When shutdown arrived the plant was in "its best stock position in years," another testimony to the improved relationships between staff and manufacturing.

MANUFACTURING AND ENGINEERING: The relation of manufacturing and engineering improved in many ways during this period. In July and August a number of task groups were established. On a given project all areas of the plant were to be represented by the most informed and qualified men. These projects increased the frequency of interaction between the two areas at all levels and reinforced their mutual dependence and newly acquired systems perspective. For example, in the complicated new microware system maintenance, manufacturing, quality control, and engineering all had to work together on a tight schedule. Maintenance worked with engineering on design and installation problems, manufacturing worked with engineering on design and process problems, and quality control had to work with manufacturing on standards. With all the potential problems, the project was finished on schedule and was a great success. Comments heard from both sides included "I'm finally able to get some cooperation . . . ." Both areas benefited from the success and this too furthered the increased mutual respect and worked toward more cooperation and collaboration between the two areas.

STAFF AND ENGINEERING: During the postgrid period staff and engineering increased their formal and informal contacts. Staff was included in many of the task groups (for example, the microware group) and engineering was invited to the new planning meeting. With this increase in interaction few problems arose between the two areas during the March to August 1971 period, even though this was a period of substantial engineering activity. Overall, the confusion and lack of contact between the two areas were decreased, if only because of the expanded interaction patterns and the increased spirit of plantwide collaboration.

INTRAMANUFACTURING: The intradepartmental relations in manufacturing during the last period were problematical. Both staff and engineering worked well internally, while the manufacturing area developed intradepartmental conflicts and lacked internal integration. The period from March 1971 to August 1971 reinforced the internal relationships in staff and engineering and saw a number of improvements in the manufacturing area.

Of major importance to the manufacturing area was the cut from four to two department heads and the pruning of shift foremen down to eight. With a stable work load, this cut again increased the responsibility of the manufacturing men. During the period in question a number of other changes happened in manufacturing. The interaction between shift foremen and department heads increased with the initiation of daily meetings, which were more active, open, and lively than the previous manufacturing meetings had been. The communication between the two levels increased and became more mutual as the managers strove to use their new grid skills. The effect was also present at the daily meeting between Smith and his department heads.

With the increase in overall work load on the manufacturing men, the shift foremen were finally given real authority and responsibility by their department heads. Shift foremen worked from their own budgets and were given total responsibility for their own areas. The department heads had to take a longer work perspective and as such had to get involved in task groups and other planning-oriented work. By July 1971 a department head noted that the manufacturing area was "properly meshed and finally working as a team. . . ." He noted the increase in interactions within the area, especially between the shift foremen. The collaboration between the hot and cold ends was enhanced by the close working relation of the two department heads and the expanded interaction and communication between the shift foremen.

As the individuals in all levels and areas of the plant became more mobile, spans of cognitions increased and interpersonal skills improved; the problem of lack of integration decreased. For instance, as the manufacturing men began to understand the importance and problems of engineering and began to interact with the engineers themselves, previous misconceptions and hostilities decreased. Within the manufacturing area integration increased as shift foremen were finally given greater information in terms of budgets and established goals. They were also given the responsibility and authority to work with the hourly employees and among themselves.

There were still real differences in the degree of openness to people of higher status, and individuals often returned to their old styles in time of crisis. Yet, when one compares postgrid to the pregrid period, it becomes obvious that the plant was a very different place by August 1971. Where before there had been structural differentiation complicated by lack of integration and information distortion, by August the differentiated areas were better integrated, with a much more diffuse and accurate flow of information in both vertical and horizontal directions. Where before there was hesitation to delegate and inability to take advantage of new responsibilities, by August the men at Becket had a new and common technique, language, and attitude towards work and responsibility. This new culture emphasized honesty, openness, problem confronting and delegation of decision making to the level of most information and responsibility. While this kind of behavioral change was exactly what the top team desired and reinforced, it also paid off for the men. This new operating style had quite observable effects on the plant productivity, thus reflecting well on the men who made it happen. By July the productivity figure reached an all-time high of $10.38, compared with the 1970 average of $7.80. The gross margin figure increased by 12.8 percent during the period in question, compared to 1.8 percent in the previous year. Consistent with the productivity indications of plant effectiveness were the observation by many that the usually troublesome periods before and after shutdown went "the smoothest they have ever gone . . ." and the fact that, while more problems were being brought up, the number of fires reaching the top team decreased.

The period from March to August 1971 saw the culture of the plant move to one that Freeman and the top team had been stressing since the previous summer. While the transition to the new ideology was not perfect, by August Becket had evolved into a very dynamic and responsive plant. Stability is not part of the Boise culture. By mid-August the whole top team had been reshuffled, but this sudden change and its effects are another paper.

CHAPTER 3

# INTEGRATION AND IMPLICATIONS

The last chapter has described Becket over forty-two months in terms of the perceptions of its employees and the observations of the researcher. Each functional area of the plant and its relation with the other areas was described for each of four periods. The periods can be outlined and summarized in the following way:

|  | *Period* |
|---|---|
| January 1968 to January 1970, Mitchell, plant manager; environmental change; the plant, "fat and lazy" | 1 |
| January 1970 to April 1970, Freeman to plant manager; development of top team, ideological and structural changes | 2 |
| April 1970 to March 1971, response to the changes: lack of plantwide integration, insecurity, internal integration except for manufacturing | 3 |
| April 1971 to August 1971, behavioral changes: increased integration, collaboration, and plant effectiveness | 4 |

Before the process of change at Becket can be conceptualized, it must be firmly established that Becket did actually change. Was the 1971 Becket plant indeed different from 1968? To answer this question the patterns of interactions will be summarized for three different periods over the forty-two months. The time periods will be January 1968 to April 1970 (T1, T2), April 1970 to April 1971 (T3), and April 1971 to August 1971 (T4). The patterns of interactions within and between the functional areas and with the plant manager will be summarized in terms of both the direction and frequency of contact (Lawrence, 1958; Whyte, 1951a; Guest, 1962).

## JANUARY 1968 TO APRIL 1970 (T1, T2)

The period during Mitchell's term as plant manager, which ends with the changes initiated by Freeman, is the base line for this case study and is quite simple to review.

INTERDEPARTMENTAL RELATIONS: Manufacturing with the direct aid of the plant manager completely dominated the plant. At all levels, the direction of influence was manufacturing to engineering or staff. The frequency of interaction between members of the three areas was low and typically of a win–lose variety. There were no regular formal meetings set up between manufacturing and engineering or between engineering and staff. These groups met only during monthly meetings or during crisis situations. Manufacturing and staff did meet once a week at the "planning meeting." This meeting was regular but did very little planning. Interaction between various areas was limited to the department head level and above. The contact between shift foremen and engineers or staff was very rare and the contact between lower-level men in one department and higher-level men in other areas was nonexistent. The interdepartmental situation is summarized in Chart 4.

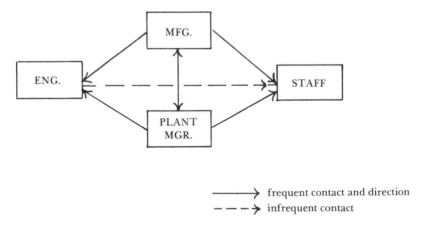

⟶ frequent contact and direction

– – –⟶ infrequent contact

*Chart 4: Interdepartmental Patterns of Interaction, January 1968 to April 1970 (T1, T2).*

MANUFACTURING: Within the manufacturing area the relationships were one way between levels and infrequent and strained within levels. The patterns of interactions can be summarized: (A) Both Bob Smith and Mitchell sent directions to the seven department heads. Often the directions were contradictory. The department heads interacted more with Mitchell than with Smith and felt they could influence him more. This effect extended to the shift foremen also. (B) Between department heads the frequency of contact was limited to manufacturing meetings. Their relationships were characterized as win–lose. Each man worked to keep his area straight; thus, internal coordination was poor. (C) The relations between department heads and shift foremen were generally initiated by the department head. The influence was always from superior to subordinate. Interactions between department heads and shift foremen in their areas were high because there was close supervision. Interaction between department heads and shift foremen in other areas was rare. (D) Interactions between shift foremen were frequent and mutual within a particular process area. Interactions between shift foremen in other departments in the plant were very infrequent.

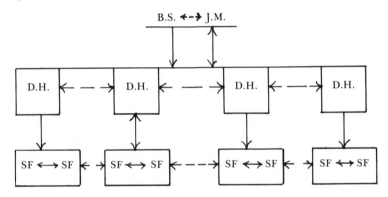

*Chart 5: Patterns of Interaction, Manufacturing (T1, T2)*

STAFF: The staff area was primarily moved by manufacturing. Manufacturing's influence was transmitted through the expediters on a

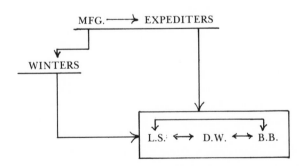

*Chart 6: Patterns of Interaction, Staff (T1, T2)*

day-to-day basis and to Paul Winters at the planning meeting. Within the department Winters kept all the responsibility and gave all the instructions. The frequency of contact between the schedulers and purchasers was high. The managers also received day-to-day directions from the expediters. The patterns are summarized in Chart 6.

ENGINEERING: Before the arrival of John Brown, engineering was virtually nonexistent at Becket and the engineers' internal dynamics reflected their lack of organization.

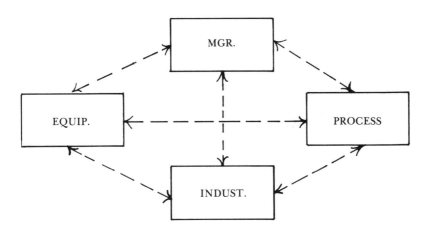

*Chart 7: Patterns of Interaction, Engineering (T1, T2)*

No lines are drawn in Chart 7 since each manager worked within his area. The lack of lines do not reflect conflict but an absence of work-related relationships.

PLANT MANAGER AND TOP MANAGERS: During his stay as plant manager, Mitchell established very definite relationships with the various areas. Because his previous job had been production superintendent, Mitchell was most influenced by the manufacturing area. Mitchell was also strongly influenced by the union and the hourly employees. He did not have real ties with either staff or engineering. Within these areas influence was unidirectional, with the top managers acting individually and with no team identification.

*57*

ORGANIZATIONAL CHANGE

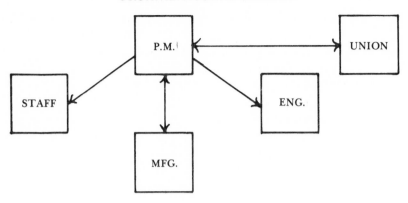

*Chart 8: Patterns of Interaction, Top Managers (T1, T2)*

In all, the patterns of interactions throughout the plant during this period can be described as unilateral with the superiors initiating to the subordinates. The manufacturing area exerted the most influence in the plant and contact between areas was infrequent. The amount of interaction of lower-level men anywhere was minimal except within their own work area. While these patterns of interaction did cause some dissatisfaction at the lower and middle levels, the structure was very stable, a product of the good economy during the 1960s.

## APRIL 1970 TO APRIL 1971 (T3)

This period was one of dramatic changes at Becket. During this time the structural changes at Becket began to have great impact on the patterns of interactions that had been so stable during the previous period.

INTERDEPARTMENTAL RELATIONS: During this year the interdepartmental relations changed. No longer did manufacturing completely dominate the plant, Engineering was given a greater budget and increased influence, and staff was chartered to direct manufacturing. This equalization in influence necessitated that all three areas establish contact; yet, the exhortations of Freeman and his team did little to alleviate the conflict, confusion, and tension between the three areas. Frequency of contact increased only at the department-head level. The direction of influence was confused as each department tried to adjust to its new position. Below the department-head level, the frequency of contact remained very low, as each area withdrew to take care of its own enlarged responsibilities. During this period Freeman did not exert direct influence on any of the three areas.

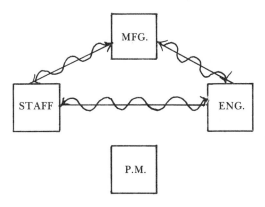

*Chart 9: Interdepartmental Patterns of Interaction, April 1970 to April 1971 (T3)*

MANUFACTURING: Within manufacturing, the loss in influence and the decrease in the numbers of department heads and shift foremen increased tension and insecurity. Each of the four areas withdrew into its own tasks. The relations within and between levels can be reviewed: (A) Smith took total responsibility for the manufacturing floor. His relations with the department heads was mostly unilateral only because the department heads did not take advantage of the opportunity to use their influence. Smith met with his department heads once a day. (B) Within the hot and cold ends, the department heads increased their contact and the direction was mutual. Contact between the ends was less frequent and more strained. (C) The relationships between department heads and shift

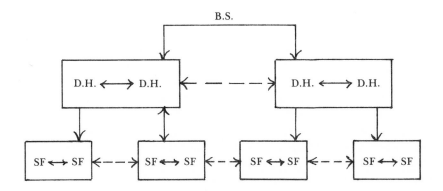

*Chart 10: Patterns of Interaction, Manufacturing (T3)*

foreman remained unilateral even with encouragements to the contrary by Freeman and Smith. (D) The relationships between shift foremen within an area were frequent and cooperative. Outside of their areas the contacts remained limited, especially with men outside the manufacturing areas.

ENGINEERING: With the arrival of Brown the engineering group radically changed. Brown developed a coordinated and ambitious department and stressed communication and cooperation between the subareas. Frequency of interaction between all areas in engineering was increased with the formation of many formal meetings and task groups. Two-way influence was encouraged. Brown constantly stressed the virtues of openness, honesty, and conflict resolution. Outside the area the contacts remained limited. Engineering's relation with manufacturing was conflict ridden, while with staff it was generally confused and infrequent.

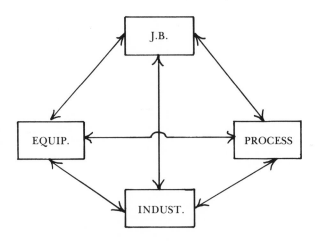

*Chart 11: Patterns of Interaction, Engineering (T3)*

STAFF: With the arrival of Mazur and the changes initiated by Freeman and his team, the staff area reordered its internal relations. Mazur gave L.S. and D.W. total responsibility for scheduling and purchasing respectively. Mazur also stressed the need for internal coordination and contact at all levels. Outside of the staff area, relations were infrequent and confused with engineering and strained with manufacturing.

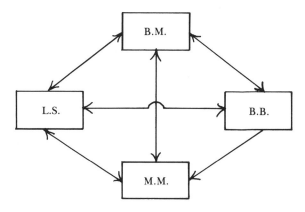

*Chart 12: Patterns of Interaction, Staff (T3)*

FREEMAN AND THE TOP TEAM: The year saw the emergence of the top level managers and Freeman as a team. Freeman was both the formal and informal leader of the top team. The group met as a whole approximately three times a month, although they met informally each day. The direction of interaction was two-way within the team, except for Freeman's differential influence.

In all, the most changes in interaction patterns during the period April 1970 to April 1971 were internal to the areas. In each area the frequency of interactions increased and became more bilateral. The exception was in manufacturing. There the interactions between the hot and cold ends remained low and confused while the intraend relationships improved at the department head level. Between the functional areas the interaction remained low and of a poor quality. There remained little or no contact between lower-level monthly employees in the three areas.

## APRIL 1971 TO AUGUST 1971 (T4)

The behavioral interventions during this period primarily affected interdepartmental and intramanufacturing problems; therefore, only these areas will be discussed.

INTERDEPARTMENTAL RELATIONS: During this period the systems orientation constantly espoused by the top team began to have an effect. The interactions between all three areas increased and tended to be of a give-and-take-nature. This was true at all levels as formal meetings and task groups were established. Individual mobility in the plant also reinforced this effect. While there were "relapses," the basic patterns of interaction between the areas are described by Chart 13.

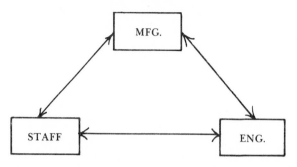

*Chart 13: Interdepartmental Patterns of Interaction, April 1971 to August 1971 (T4)*

MANUFACTURING: Within manufacturing the direction and frequency of interaction became more mutual and increased. This process was hastened by the decrease in department heads and shift foremen. Cooperation between the hot and cold ends was increased, relations between department heads and shift foremen improved, and relationships between shift foremen increased in frequency and quality. See Chart 14.

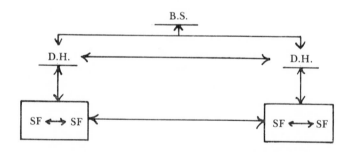

*Chart 14: Patterns of Interaction, Manufacturing (T4)*

By August 1971 the patterns of interactions throughout the plant were markedly different from those in January 1970 and April 1971. There were a greater number of interactions and they were of a higher quality in terms of openness, conflict resolution, and trust within and between all areas. Becket was indeed a "different kind of place" by August 1971.

INTEGRATION

Given the fact that Becket changed dramatically over the forty-two months the question shifts to the basic matters of this study. What was the process of change at Becket and how can we conceptualize the dynamics of such a complex process? Were the changes caused by the economy, Freeman, the grid, or some combination of the three? To answer these questions this section is divided into two phases, pre- and postgrid. The discussion of the process of change occurring within each time frame will follow. Like the case study, the division into time periods is arbitrary and unreal. The phases were interdependent and overlapped one another; yet, the process can best be conceptualized separately. The pregrid section will describe ideological and structural changes, while the postgrid section will describe behavioral (reeducational) changes at Becket. This section will conclude with some alternative and competing explanations to that of the structural-behavioral integration.

PREGRID: This portion, discussing the processes of Becket to April 1971, will cover Times One, Two, and Three of Chapter Two. Time One described Becket with Mitchell as plant manager. During this period conditions developed that led to the promotion of Freeman. Becket was a plant on the tail end of a period of high prosperity, yet had declining organizational health and effectiveness. Times Two and Three saw changes in personnel, work loads, relations of power and authority and environment.

Probably the primary factor behind the promotion of Freeman was the inability of Becket to cope with or adapt to its new environment under the direction of Mitchell. By 1968 the falling economy in the country had begun to effect Becket directly. From 1968 to 1970, orders and volume declined at a rate of approximately 4 percent per year. At the same time, total plant dollar volume did not increase. Productivity at the end of 1969 reached 7.67, a modest 1.5 percent increase over the previous year. The arrival of Freeman did nothing to stimulate the national economy, and the trends continued throughout the year. Productivity during 1970 rose to 7.80, and increase of 1.8 percent over 1969. Thus, although there were no economic changes for the better through March 1971, plant productivity showed a definite increment. (A note of caution: Productivity as an indication of relative plant performance is a bit misleading. It is determined by direct versus indirect labor, engineering improvements, and sales volume. All of these factors changed during this period, most importantly the level of indirect labor. Therefore, the figure of dollars per person per hour is partially confounded as an indicator of plant performance.) Employment levels decreased at a steady rate throughout the plant. By March 1971 the total number of employees at Becket was around 400, consisting of 330 hourly, 30 weekly, and 40 monthly employees. The figures at the end of 1969 were 411 hourly, 20 weekly, and 48 monthly, totaling 479.

*Ideological and Structural Change:* April 1970 to April 1971 was a period of constant flux at Becket. To sort out the multitude of changes two concepts are useful, ideological change and structural change. Ideological change refers to changes in values, norms, expectations, and criteria for success as defined and practiced by top management. Structural change, as described before, refers to changes in authority distribution, communication flow, control systems, decision-making level, and work flow.

Ideological changes began with the arrival of Freeman and the establishment of his team. Besides Freeman, five of the seven top managers were either new to Becket or new to their positions. Over the year this new team deliberately moved to change the culture of the plant. Evaluation procedures, stricter criteria for success, more ambitious goals, longer-range planning, a more systematic view of the plant, and in general a different style of management were among the ideological changes being practiced and espoused by the most important people in the plant. Associated with these new values was a definite change in the makeup of the monthly employees. There were new, young, educated people in the great majority of the most influential positions. With this influx of younger men a dramatic decrease occurred in the overall number of monthly employees. In all, the new ideology emphasized change, ambition, progress, and the notion of Becket as a "tight ship."

Three separate structural changes occurred during this period: changes in size; differentiation of staff, manufacturing, and engineering; and redistribution of influence among the three functional areas.

During the year the number of people at Becket decreased by 15 percent. Included in this pruning is the decrease in monthly employees described above. Although the number of levels remained constant, the number of men at each level decreased. This decrease forced job enlargement and combination and a lowering of the decision-making responsibility, especially in manufacturing.

During April 1970 to April 1971, Freeman and his team formally differentiated staff and engineering from manufacturing. The new charters of the three areas were spelled out distinctly. Staff was to be responsible for budgets, planning, and scheduling, while engineering was to be responsible for innovation over and above its firefighting duties.

Related to the formal differentiation of the areas was a decrease in the influence manufacturing had in the plant and a concomitant increase for both staff and engineering. While manufacturing remained the leading system at Becket, the large power differential of the past was lessened.

*Effects:* If a systems approach to organizations has merit, then the ideological and structural changes above ought to have had extra consequences for the system as a whole. That is, one should expect effects in the plant over and above the changes themselves. At Becket the systems response was dysfunctional from an organizational point of view.

The pruning of the work force, with the increase in work load and responsibility, combined with the new expectations and demands of the young and ambitious top team to have real consequences for the management at Becket. The reaction to this new culture was one of insecurity. Most men below the top-team level were scared. The insecurity and tension arose from two areas of uncertainty. One source, most prevalent with the younger men, was the real possibility of their jobs being eliminated. Among the older men the most prevalent source was the fear and hesitation regarding changing their personal work styles in order to handle the increased expectations and load. Both sources were exacerbated by the bleak prospects for other employment outside of Becket and the reality of seeing men laid off.

Related to the insecurity was the narrowing of plant perspective during the year. If the individual had a limited span of cognition before, by April 1971 it had decreased even further. The consciousness of the other's problems and the general interdependence of the plant, although stressed by the top team, seemed to be repressed by the men and their respective departments. The result of the increased tension and exacerbated myopia was a decrease in interdepartmental communication, collaboration, and general interaction frequency. Members of each group set out to do their own jobs and "let the other guys take care of their own problems . . . ."

Besides these common plant problems, manufacturing had its own. Because of its size and internal differentiation, the manufacturing department experienced problems within its area analogous to those noted between functional areas. Relations between the hot and cold ends were poor as each department head and his shift foremen worked for his end only. Between the two ends and levels in the hierarchy time perspectives were short, interactions infrequent, and mutual problem solving rare.

Other problems can be more directly traced to the structural changes in the plant. The differentiation of the areas and the redistribution of influence was a source of much role ambiguity and role conflict between the areas as each tried to adapt to its new charter. Manufacturing had to respond to a lowering of influence, while staff and engineering had to respond to an increase in influence with their new mandates. The interdepartmental collaboration during this period was poor as each area preferred to work internally. Another effect of the structural changes was a redistribution of authority and span of control in each department. This kind of reorientation was also pushed by the top team. For example, in manufacturing the decrease in shift foremen and department heads required new work relationships. Old patterns of interaction and decision-making techniques could not get the work done as effectively as possible. The department heads were encouraged to take on more area responsibilities and at the same time to delegate decisions to their subordinates. This necessary redistribution of work and authority had two potential problem areas in the plant. In order for this redistribution to take place, the department head first had to realize that he could not continue to handle the increased load and that he must delegate some of the extra responsibility. Second, the lower-level manager must have been able to take this authority and work with it. In manufacturing some of the department heads were reluctant to give up some of their extra authority. Old work methods and personal pride were particularly hard to change in the manufacturing area even with increased work loads. The second problem was more prevalent and could be observed throughout the plant. With an increase in responsibility and work load, the lower-level monthly employee found that he had to change his previous operating style. He had to make more decisions and interact with many more people than before. Often he needed the cooperation of people outside of his department. The general lack of plant perspective, interpersonal skills, and problem-solving abilities caused much conflict and inefficiency between managers and increased individual feelings of insecurity.

The effects of the ideological and structural changes over the year showed up in different ways both positive and negative. While there was more appropriate differentiation between the areas, there was poor integration. While there was often an increase in the delegation of authority and responsibility to lower levels in the organization, many men at those levels did not know how to use them effectively. Finally, while there was a strong desire by the top team to make Becket a more effective plant, the reaction of many monthly and hourly employees to the new expectations and manning levels was one of increasing insecurity and uncertainty. To attack the problems of poor plant perspective, poor integration, lack of communication and trust, and to reinforce the managerial orientations of the top team, the grid program was initiated. April 1971 saw the first Becket group "go to school."

POSTGRID: From April 1971 to August 1971 the economic environment continued its decrease at the rate of 4 percent per year and layoffs continued at the plant. By August the plant figures were 315 hourly, 37 monthly, and 29 weekly employees, for a total of 381, a decrease of 20 percent from January 1970. The decreases were mostly from the hourly levels. During the year layoffs from the monthly ranks lessened as the plant reached "understaffed levels." As a result, job insecurity because of job elimination decreased, while insecurity because of job evaluation increased. Insecurity ran high until after the grid sessions. There were no new changes in the top team. The most notable figure for this period was the dramatic increase in productivity. By August 1971 the productivity figure had jumped to 10.38, a 12.8 percent increase over the January 1 figure of 7.80, which compares well with a 1.8 percent increase during 1970 and a 1.5 percent increase during 1969.

*Behavioral Change:* April 1971 was the beginning of school for Becket management. Unlike the structural changes outlined above, the behavioral changes were taken from a packaged organizational development program. The whole management team participated in Phase One of the Blake and Mouton managerial grid, although the participants were not limited to Becket employees. Three sessions were held over two months. The essence of the Phase One program is education, or more properly reeducation. The week-long seminar exposed the men to a different set of work norms, values, and skills. Blake and Mouton write: "[Phase One] serves more as a trigger which creates a readiness to really work on human problems of management" (Blake *et al.*, 1964: 137). More specifically, in Phase One the managers participated in instrumental grid seminars conducted by line managers. The sessions for Becket were run by Frank O'Connor and Carl Hoffman and included men from all over the Boise system. The total group of forty to forty-five men was broken up, on a diagonal-slice basis (that is, from different levels and areas), into groups of ten to twelve. The learning was conceptual and systematic, involving study, lectures, and experiential investigation of individual and group behavior. Also, in specific portions of the program each member evaluated his own work behavior in terms of the principles learned. Goals for the seminar included increased clarity of approaches for solving production and people problems, more open listening and candid speaking, greater understanding of how to use critique methods, reduction in self deception, and improved understanding of intergroup dynamics.

In all, Phase One is a program that attempts to teach new language, norms, and values to the participants. With these new work values are also taught complementary interpersonal and intergroup skills. Throughout, the program's pragmatic value, its potential as a tool, was constantly reinforced. The increase in individual work responsibility, the lack of integration within and between areas, and importance of the week as defined by the top team combined to make the Becket managers receptive students.

*Effects:* Given the decrease in the structural changes and the fact that the economy and environment remained unchanged, inspection of the April 1971 and August 1971 interaction charts leads to the conclusion that the behavioral intervention had a marked effect on the plant. The behavioral knowledge and skills (for example, systems perspective, critiquing) gained from Phase One not only were vigorously reinforced by Freeman and his team, but also fit very well with the altered organizational structure.

Throughout the plant one could observe the increased quality of meetings, the increased frequency of interactions, the increased mutuality of influence, more confronting, and more problem solving at lower levels. With the increased awareness of Becket as a system, department heads used their new skills to begin to resolve "long-standing mutual problems." The increased mobility at the lower managerial levels also contributed to the amelioration of the interdepartmental strain and confusion. With their enlarged plant perspective the department heads took on different approaches to their jobs (for example, task groups) and delegated more of their day-to-day responsibility to their shift foremen. Daily meetings were initiated between department heads and shift foremen to increase intradepartmental dialogue. Improved interpersonal skills were especially noticeable at the shift-foremen level. To complement their increased responsibility, the shift foremen were more aggressive in demanding more access to information. By June the shift foremen began establishing effective relations with others around the plant. While the frequency of crises was believed to have increased, the solutions were developed at these lower levels. All the improvements in interpersonal and intergroup skills worked towards integration between the three functional areas and within the manufacturing area. The productivity results served to decrease the evaluation apprehension and reflected the new fit between the social structure, the groups, and the individuals at Becket. In August Becket entered shutdown in "the best shape we've been in for years . . . ."

SOME OTHER INTERPRETATIONS: While this section has conceptualized the changes at Becket in terms of a combination of structural and behavioral changes, at least five competing explanations can be offered given the data. These explanations can be divided into those involving lag effects and those involving cathartic and unfreezing effects. The lag explanations can be further subdivided into three explanations of the changes observed at Becket: structural change alone was sufficient to explain the results, Freeman and his team were sufficient, and a lessening of insecurity given the Phase One experience (a sort of "investment in me" rationale).

The cathartic interpretations can be divided into two further explanations of changes at Becket. The positive plant dynamics resulted not from skills and cognitive learning during Time Four but from an opportunity to vent frustration or to share common troubles. Since the case had no controls, no final or complete conclusions can be drawn. The structural-behavioral explanation can only be defended as the most plausible explanation given the data at hand or on intuitive grounds (Phillips, 1970).

The lag explanations imply that the Phase One session and the follow-up at the plant may have been irrelevant. These explanations must hold that the changes at Becket would have occurred without Phase One. The cathartic explanations reject the skill development and learning aspect of the grid program. These explanations rely on an increased motivation to do a better job as the result of the week away. The alternative that the behavioral changes alone affected the plant irrespective of the structural changes will be discussed later.

Were the results found by August 1971 a result of the structural changes alone? Were the effects a result of Freeman and his team alone?

Both explanations would have to say that the increased interaction patterns, new language, altered meeting behaviors, and so on would have occurred without the grid session. Did the new role definitions and structural requirements finally force the men into the new behaviors? Possibly the managers finally received the message from Freeman and his men and behaved accordingly or maybe Freeman's charisma alone finally forced the managers to behave as he desired. Yet considering the full year (Period three) in which the structural changes and the exhortations of Freeman and his team had little effect on these kinds of process variables, the jump needed for this lag explanation is great. As shown, even with Freeman's desire for a more integrated plant, the year April 1970 to April 1971 saw the plantwide integration decrease. While one could argue that over time either the structural changes or the top team desires would have accomplished the changes as described, this rationale is clearly not acceptable given the sudden shift in plant integration (Period Four). Another explanation of the lag effect is more difficult to argue against. Possibly the major changes brought by Freeman and his team (Period Two) so threw the plant out of equilibrium that it took a full year for the system to adjust. With the new equilibrium plant performance increased and plant integration improved.

The managers' possible rationale that the pruning was finished and that top management was investing in the tightened team (survivors) relies on increased security as a motivating force. If the men were more secure they could perform more effectively, grid or no grid. This explanation is specious since, as mentioned in the text (pp. 46-47), the insecurity actually increased before and during grid. While *job elimination* did decrease, job evaluation *increased*. It was only after the grid program was completed and plant effectiveness improved that the overall security factor became less worrisome to the men. In all, the explanations based on the irrelevance of the grid program are not as convincing as the dual explanation given the development of the plant over the months in question.

If, however, one is willing to grant some effects of the Phase One week, can one be sure that the positive plant dynamics resulted from new skills and cognitive learning or were they a result of men getting together and sharing their troubles? These explanations assume that the skills, language, and meeting behaviors found after the grid week (Period Four) were not substantive and unique aspects of the grid but rather were results of men being motivated or more free to do a better job and use preexisting skills.

More specifically, the explanations that the men "blew off some steam" or that they remet each other under nonstressful conditions and shared common experiences and troubles cannot be discounted. These explanations assume that after the grid experience the men returned to the plant free to use skills and techniques that they had always had yet rarely used. These explanations undoubtedly explain part of the postgrid results. If, however, one says that the grid did not teach the men new skills or techniques, the many newfound behaviors (for example, increased confronting, new language, systems perspective, team building) must then be explained as skills previously existing in the manager's repertoire. This is stretching the point, especially since these behaviors and attitudes were not evident before the grid week and even were mentioned by interviewees as essential managerial deficiencies before the grid sessions were initiated. Thus, while the men did have a chance to voice their frustrations and enjoy each others' company on plant time, the case suggests that the men did in fact come away from Phase One with skills, ideas, and a language that they did not have before. Here, Freeman's influence cannot be underestimated. Once these new skills were used they were vigorously reinforced by the most influential men in the plant. This reinforcement further highlighted the pragmatic aspect of grid at Becket.

Given the nature of the research at Becket no firm conclusions can be reached. No explanation can be shown to be conclusive, but explanations can be better or worse in fitting the data collected. It is the author's opinion that the structural-behavioral explanation is the most parsimonious and most plausible given the data.

## PROCESS OF CHANGE

The process of change at Becket as described in the previous sections followed a temporal sequence conceptually divided into two phases: ideological and structural changes followed by behavioral change. In terms of the literature review and the debate on the either-or approach to change, the Becket experience suggests the efficacy of a dual strategy. At this point, we can look back and discuss the four potential strategies for change and hypothesize as to their potential consequences. Assume throughout this discussion that top management (ideological) support is a given. Indeed, most theorists agree that this support is required for any successful change program (Katz and Kahn, 1966; Blake and Mouton, 1964; Beckhard, 1969; Argyris, 1962).

STRUCTURAL CHANGE ALONE: Structural change at Becket did not yield, in the year observed, an effective organization. Rather, each functional area withdrew into itself. The changes in expectations and role requirements were not responded to at the individual or group level. After a year the plant was characterized as tense and insecure, even with the increase in productivity. In Likert's terminology, the intervening variables, such as attitudes and satisfaction, were in an unstable condition (Likert, 1967). In more abstract terms, the structural interventions changed role definitions, relationships, and expectations. While role ambiguity was small, the ability to communicate or to carry out the new tasks was problematical. The sudden shift in role structure, relationships, and functional requirements for the job led directly to role conflict and the resultant organizational inefficiency and individual stress (Kahn et al., 1964).

BEHAVIORAL CHANGE ALONE: Behavioral change alone was not attempted at Becket, but we can hypothesize as to its effects. It is the author's position that if the men had gone to Phase One without structural support at the plant none of the new behaviors or skills would have been possible. With Becket's structure and routine, the values and norms learned at grid would have been incongruent. Given Becket's size, lack of differentiation, power concentration, and decision-making level, the new techniques could not have been reinforced. For example, with an unchanged distribution of influence, staff and engineering could not have been successful in their tasks even with new interpersonal skills. With seven department heads and twenty-five shift foremen in manufacturing, the desire for increased responsibility or decision making could not have been met. The effects of this lack of skill reinforcement at home have been aptly summarized by Katz and Kahn (1966:426), "Unless a person is assigned responsibility for decision making, all the training of individual or of small groups to utilize group processes . . . [is] likely to be transitory or even abortive." In all, it is a safe conclusion that behavioral change alone would have suffered the familiar transfer-home problem (Harrison, 1962, Campbell and Dunnette, 1968; and Friedlander, 1967).

STRUCTURAL, THEN BEHAVIORAL, CHANGE: This approach was used at Becket with the positive results described before. With long-term goals established and the relevant information available, Freeman and team initiated structural changes. Then a behavioral intervention was used to enhance plant integration. With this sequencing, role conflicts of the structural intervention were attacked with group educational methods. This technique improved communication flow and interpersonal relations and cleared role ambiguity. In terms of role theory, this strategy first affects the role networks and role sets and then socializes the entire team with complementary skills and work-related values.

BEHAVIORAL, THEN STRUCTURAL, CHANGE: This approach is similar in sequence to the Blake and Mouton six-phase program. The rationale is that behavioral changes are necessary first to improve interpersonal skills, problem solving, and general plant culture. Once educated, the organization is then able effectively to plan and change its structure. At Becket this approach probably would not have been as effective as the structural-behavioral sequencing for two reasons. Most important, given the certainty of the task, was the fact that the relevant information was located with Freeman and his team. To disperse the decision would violate norms of decision-making locus and would not have added to the information content of the decision (Katz and Kahn, 1966; March and Simon, 1958). Of less theoretical significance is the fact that the managers would have had to define themselves out of jobs. Given the outside work environment that would have been an unlikely decision. In general though, whether this approach has consequences different from those of the reverse approach is an untested question. A critical factor in the comparison is not whether either strategy produces change, but which strategy is most effective.

In all, the Becket case demonstrates the efficacy of the systems approach to organizational change. Structural change alone was not effective and a case was made showing why behavioral change alone would also not have been effective. Yet the sequencing of structural then complementary behavioral change was found to be successful. The behavioral then structural approach, although probably not an effective strategy for Becket, remains a general question. In retrospect, neither approach alone could be considered sufficient given Becket as the organization. A dual approach was necessary.

The results of the Becket experience are corroborating evidence for the systematic approach to planned change as discussed in Chapter One. With the analysis and integration of the case completed are there any hypotheses to be postulated? Given the literature review and the case material, two hypotheses do suggest themselves. The first hypothesis is quite broad but is a necessary first proposition: In general *a dual approach is a more effective change strategy than either structural or behavioral change taken alone.* The Becket experience suggests an elaboration of this general proposition: *In an organization with a certain technology, structural-behavioral sequencing is a more effective change strategy than either approach taken alone.*

Other questions then arise. If, in general, both approaches are necessary, does the sequencing matter? Why was the structural-behavioral approach so effective at Becket? The next section will speculate on the questions raised above and others concerned with systematic change strategies.

## TOWARD A CONTINGENCY APPROACH TO ORGANIZATIONAL CHANGE

With this sample of one, the combination of structural followed by behavioral change was found to be an effective strategy for change. Larger more encompassing questions can now be asked. On what other kinds of organizations would the same strategy have worked? Certainly the most effective technique at Becket is not the one best way. Also, is the sequencing important and if so by what criteria can one determine the most effective strategy?

A primary purpose of exploratory research is to generate hypotheses for future testing, but in this case we can go further than isolated hypothesis generation. It has been suggested by Glaser and Strauss (1967) and Phillips (1971) that in underdeveloped fields, exploratory research ought to develop hypotheses, insight, and *theory*. Rather than developing hypotheses that will fit some existing theory or be isolated and connected to no theory at all, the researcher should generate "grounded theory" from the data (see Appendix II). A basic model to work from provides many economies. Given a theoretical model with the important variables and concepts specified, hypotheses can be generated and tested. The results can then be used to modify the model further. In this fashion the literature review and the results of the Becket experience will be used to develop a set of hypotheses for organizational change. The hypotheses derived will include the results from the preceding section. In line with this theory-hypothesis-modification process the first task is briefly to outline a model for organizational change. From there a number of hypotheses on organizational change will be derived. The assumption here is that there are underlying patterns of change strategies. The ecclectic approach to change (Huse and Beer, 1971) violates scientific postulates of orderliness. Also, though, the notion of underlying patterns of change strategies must assume that the social world demands more differentiated approaches than the simplistic approaches discussed in Chapter One (Thompson, 1967). This section then, will present the essentials of a contingency approach to organizational change.

Chapter One introduced technology as a potentially important variable for organizational change. Here, technology will be used as a critical variable for a contingency model of organizational change. Since the work of Burns and Stalker (1961) the importance of technology and task have been extensively studied. The area of organizational design has received much attention from the rash of research done on the relation of organizational structure to technology (Thompson, 1967; Woodward, 1965; Lawrence and Lorsch, 1967; Perrow, 1970; and Mohr, 1971). This research has shown that an organization must match technology and structure to be effective. It has been found that organizations with uncertain (nonroutine) technologies must be structured organically. In an organic system there is low specificity of role description, little reliance on formal rules, pervasive communication flow, and a low level of decision making. Organizations with certain (routine) technologies, on the other hand, must be structured mechanistically. Mechanistic systems are characterized by high specificity of role description, high reliance on rules, use of a communication hierarchy, and high-level decision making. A number of researchers have found these results; yet, a common problem exists. The problem is that technology and task are not used comparably by each researcher. For instance Lawrence and Lorsch use "dynamic or uncertain environment," Woodward used "technique of production," and Perrow the "degree of routinization" of the task. Galbreith has analyzed much of the previous literature on organizational technologies and environment and has determined that a key factor is the predictability of the task on which the organization is working. The greater the predictability (certainty) the more formal the rules, the greater the number of levels in the hierarchy, and the higher the level at which decisions are made. Conversely, the results are reversed in organizations where the task is less predictable, as more information must be processed at all levels for the decisions to be made and the job done (Galbreith, 1969, 1973).

The notion of complexity in the technical process and its relation to organizational structure has been furthered by Thompson's work (1967). Thompson postulates a direct relation between problems of coordination, interdependence, and technological complexity. He distinguishes among three types of interdependence: pooled, sequential, and reciprocal. Pooled or generalized interdependence is coordinated by standardization and is least costly in terms of communication flow and decision effort, while sequential interdependence is coordinated by planning. Reciprocal interdependence, the most complex, must be coordinated by mutual adjustment and is the most demanding in terms of communication flow and difficulty of decisions. Thus, the more complex the technology, the greater is the strain for effective coordination and the reliance on communication flow and information processing. Udy (1965) reaches similar conclusions. He observes that both vertical and horizontal communications increase as the "degree of mechanization" of the technical process decreases. Further, he notes that the reliance on expertise increases and is found lower in the organization as the degree of mechanization decreases.

The work on organizational design will be the core of the contingency theory presented here. The jump from organizational design to organizational change is not dramatic. The primary variable, from Galbreith, is task predictability and its correlates of level of hierarchy, role reliance, and information flow. While all of these correlates are influential in determining the culture of an organization, information level and flow are most important variables concerning organizational-change strategies because behavioral and structural changes must be based on relevant and accurate knowledge of the task and its processes (Weick, 1969:40-42).

The task certainty and information-flow perspective on organizational design suggests that organizational-change strategies ought to be different in organizations with different kinds of tasks. One would expect that the task predictability is a mediating variable for change programs just as it is for organizational design. From the information flow and task certainty approach, a number of hypotheses suggest themselves (top-management support is assumed throughout). The first hypothesis follows directly from above. The expectation is that the best change strategy for mechanistic organizations will be systematically different from the best change strategy for organic organizations. More formally, *organizational change efforts will be systematically different depending on the degree of predictability of the primary task.*

The next hypothesis is less general and can be seen as both induced from the data and deduced from the literature review. If organizations are conceptualized as role systems, the structural aspects of the role sets must be changed along with the individual orientations of the organizations' members. Both approaches are necessary if the organization is concerned with strategy effectiveness (Thompson, 1967). It follows then that, *under norms of effectiveness, organizational change strategies must include congruent structural and behavioral interventions.* (Congruence as used here has been discussed by Trist and Bamforth [1951] and Likert [1967].) A corollary of this hypothesis can be derived. The experience at Becket, as demonstrated in the preceding section, is especially useful here. *Dual approaches to organizational change will be more effective than either intervention alone.* Given the hypotheses of duality, the last two hypotheses address the question concerning the sequencing of the interventions which was raised before: Does the sequencing matter?

With uncertain tasks, organizational decision making is low, communication is pervasive, and information well distributed. If task equivocality is high and change therefore ambiguous, the major problem is to make the most of the system's information capacity. Behavioral skills used throughout the organization can increase the accuracy of the information flow and make for better group problem solving. While this violates Katz and Kahn's (1966) neat typology of leadership patterns and their locus in the organization, the rationale is direct. If the relevant information and competence lie lower in the system, then the top echelons are simply not able to make knowledgeable interventions. For these same reasons, those lower in the organization must be involved in more than the "use of structure" if the organization deals with uncertain technologies. The locus of the interpolation of structure (Katz and Kahn, 1966) is not invariant, but a function of the work the organization does. Given the dispersion of information, techniques must be used to bring it together most effectively (Weick, 1969). In short, under equivocal task conditions, the individual and group are hypothesized to be the prime targets for the initial intervention. It is, therefore, hypothesized that, *under norms of effectiveness, the best change sequence for systems with unpredictable tasks is behavioral followed by structural change.*

With certain tasks, organizational decision making and information is high in the organization and communication flow is restricted. Given these conditions, the information necessary to make the structural and behavioral interventions are located higher in the organizational hierarchy. These conditions permit structure to be changed first with individual or group intervention to follow. This hypothesis, the obverse of the previous one, reflects the Becket experience: *under norms of effectiveness the best change sequence for systems with predictable tasks is structural followed by behavioral change.* In answer to the question concerning the sequence of change at Becket, posed in the preceding section, it would appear that a behavioral-structural approach would not have been as effective as the reverse sequence was. The reason can be directly traced to the plant's technology, the locus of decision making, and the availability of relevant information at the plant-manager level. This sequencing hypothesis is indirectly supported in work reported by Beer and Huse (1972) and Taylor (1971). It should be emphasized here that the word "sequence" should not be taken too literally, for sequencing here means that a particular strategy (for example, the structural) should take precedence in a given period. The dual approach is an interdependent endeavor. The structural and interpersonal changes must reinforce and legitimate each other. As such, the two strategies cannot be viewed as independent interventions, but rather must be seen as different, possibly overlapping, phases in one systematic change program.

These hypotheses form the basis for a contingency approach to organizational change. There are two basic ideas here. The first is that the problem of organizational change must be attacked systematically using multiple levers. The dual strategies of structural and behavioral approaches must be used together to have maximum leverage on the system. Becket is a good example of this dual strategy. This broad dual statement can be made more specific. A case has been made that the sequencing makes a difference, which leads to the second basic idea: Different organizations, or different areas in an organization, ought to have different specific change strategies depending on the primary task.

While these hypotheses are suggestive, many unanswered questions, both practical and theoretical, remain. What is the effect of size on the process of change and on the hypotheses developed? Is timing a consideration? How stable are the changes? Can the hypotheses be generalized to voluntary or professional organizations? What about the thorny empirical problems of meaning and measurement? How are the concepts operationalized? How are the hypotheses to be more rigorously tested? What does effectiveness mean and how is it to be evaluated (Weiss and Rein, 1970)? These questions, important to the area of organizational change, await further work.

## CONCLUSIONS

The problem of social systems change is not new; yet, it is also not developed. Wilbert Moore has noted (quoted in Bennis, 1966): "The mention of 'theory of social change' will make most scientists appear defensive, furtive, guilt ridden, or frightened." Martindale writes (quoted in Bennis, 1966:99), "a leading sociologist [says] that its theory of social change is the weakest branch of sociological theory . . . ." This study has been concerned with a subset of social change, that is organizational change and its processes. Given the turbulence of the environment (Emery and Trist, 1965) and the need for organizations to adapt to new social, economic, and technological conditions (Bennis, 1969; Argyris, 1971; and U.S. Department of Health, Education and Welfare, 1973), organizational change is indeed an important and practical area; yet, one in which our knowledge is not well developed. Campbell (1971:565) makes this point strongly, "By and large, the . . . development literature is voluminous, nonempirical, nontheoretical, poorly written, and dull . . . ." He describes a process in which fads develop, gain a number of adherents, are the objects of a few empirical studies, attract a multitude of detractors, and conclude the cycle with the arrival of the next fad. The results are reflected in the change literature which to date is polarized on the structural-behavioral issue.

In reporting the process of change in a manufacturing plant over forty-two months, this study has attempted to develop some systematic hypotheses from the case and from previous literature. At the concrete level, the case itself can be of use to practitioners who find themselves faced with a declining market and increased competition. Even if not directly relevant to individual situations, the case does provide some insight into the process of change in a complex organization. This process-oriented data can only come from case studies. If nothing else, Becket alone points out that the problem of organizational adaptation requires more than simple participation in development activities. Change requires a more complex and differentiated approach.

At a more general level and more directly related to the large area of organizational change are the sections that attempt to develop hypotheses from the case. A conclusion from this broader perspective is that behavioral scientists must forget the either-or approach to change. Organizational behaviorists must begin to deal with the problems of a more differentiated and inclusive organizational change theory (Beer, in press). Technology and environment must be taken into account. To this end, this book suggests a contingency approach to change. An organizational change strategy which is successful in one situation cannot be imported to any or every other situation. The techniques for organizational change peddled by each school of thought are partly right but partly wrong. The exploratory research at Becket suggests that each approach is necessary but that neither is sufficient. The sequencing has been hypothesized to depend on technological or task conditions. This model leads one to the conclusion that it is essential to analyze the primary organizational task in order to design the most effective change strategy. The contingency model presented is one step in the theory-hypothesis generating direction. It leaves many questions unresolved and most of the work to be done. The problems of evaluation techniques and methods, effectiveness, and the effect of timing are among the many problems that must be worked out with this kind of scheme. If, however, organizations are important and if technologies and environments are changing rapidly, the area of planned organizational change cannot be ignored.

# APPENDIX I    Charts

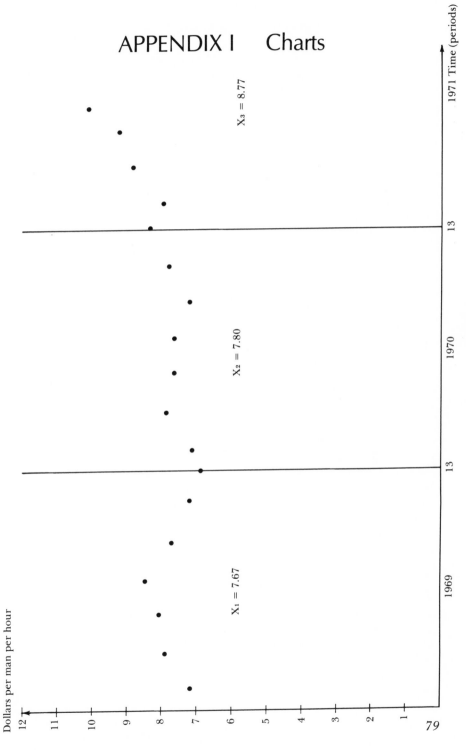

Chart A1 : Productivity

# ORGANIZATIONAL CHANGE

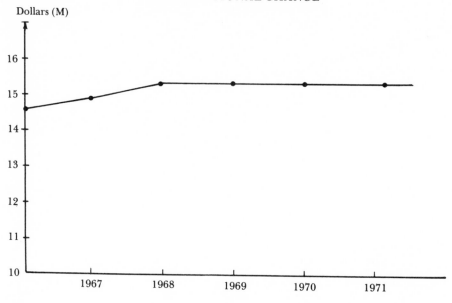

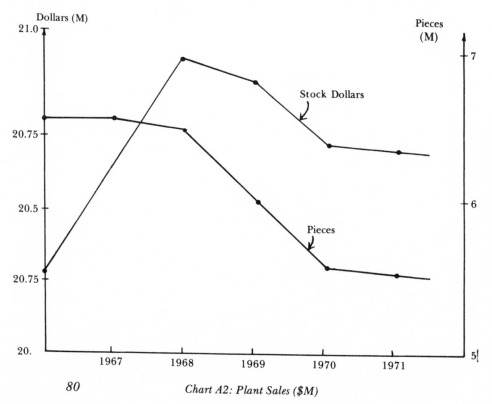

*Chart A2: Plant Sales ($M)*

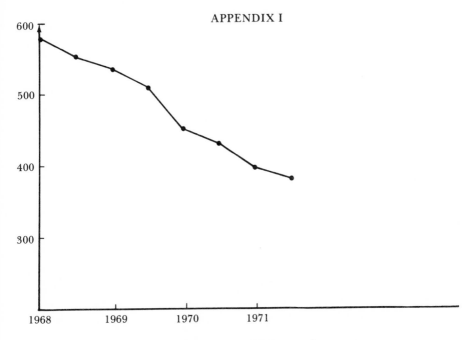

*Chart A3: Total Plant Level*

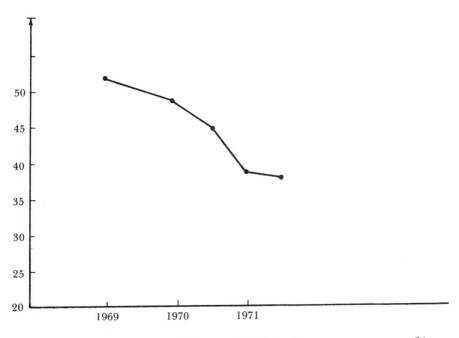

*Chart A4: Monthly Levels*

# Appendix II
# Research Strategy and Methods

That the state of knowledge regarding planned change is relatively primative has been commented upon by many, including Bennis (1966), Hornstein and his associates (1971), Zaleznick (1965), Bowers (1973), and Beer (in press). Campbell (1971) has recently reviewed the literature on organizational training and development and notes that the area of organizational change has grown atheoretically. He concludes that too much effort has been spent on techniques and methods of change at the expense of the development of conceptual models and theory of the change process. While each orientation to change can develop hypotheses, the systematic use of both structural and interpersonal approaches to change has been a neglected area. If the multiple lever approach has merit, then an interdisciplinary approach must be developed.

Given this lack of well-trodden conceptual paths to follow, exploratory work has to be done before hypotheses on organizational change can be systematically developed or tested (Walton, 1972; Glaser and Strauss, (1967). McGrath (1964) and Lachenmeyer (1970) have described very similar models of research strategy that have been useful. Both see research as a cyclical process.

McGrath's essay covers field study, experimental simulation, laboratory experiment, and computer simulation as methods for conducting organizational studies. The methods differ along a rough continuum from concrete to abstract or from a wide bandwidth-low fidelity to low bandwidth-high fidelity. Given this set of possible methods, McGrath then describes a "model for programmatic research." His model describes a process of research beginning with exploratory studies were little is known a priori and proceeding through testing, validation, and finally cross-validation in the field (McGrath, 1964). Given the state of systematic change to date, one can conclude that a viable research method for the study of organizational change at this time is the field or case study.

## FIELD STUDY

Sellitz and his associates (1959) have differentiated field methods into three types: exploratory, descriptive, and hypothesis testing. In exploratory study the primary purpose is to gain some familiarity with a problem and to develop insight and hypotheses for further research. Descriptive studies attempt to assess the characteristics of a system and to develop associative statements. Hypothesis testing centers on the collection of data that will test causal relationships. Our interest in this study is in exploratory field work, the initial step in McGrath's model. Although this study is only exploratory, it must be considered more broadly as an initial step in a continuing research process. This initial step is critical, for the most careful methods used during later stages of research are of little value if incorrect or irrelevant concepts or hypotheses are developed (Glaser and Strauss, 1967).

Exploratory field work in organizations has been termed case study, field study, or community study by various writers (Scott, 1965). The assumption is that the researcher does not know enough about the problem, a priori, to identify relevant problems or hypotheses. These must be discovered in the course of the research. To this end, in exploratory research, the investigator attempts to collect as much information on as many aspects of the situation as possible. Nothing is considered irrelevant (Becker, 1958, 1960). The focus is on the total situation. This orientation encourages the researcher to characterize the social organization with respect to the multiplicity of factors which compose it and the nature of their interdependencies. A specific technique is not the issue, but rather a particular way of organizing social observations so as to preserve the dynamics and unity of the system studied (Scott, 1965). The main emphasis in exploratory study is on the accumulation of background necessary to the development of research hypotheses and insight. The major operational characteristics of exploratory field work, thus, are flexibility and openness (Sellitz, 1959; Whyte, 1955, 1951b).

Flexibility is critical to exploratory field work. Since there are no a priori hypotheses to be tested but only a desire for exposure to reality, the data do not have built-in "sense" (Liebow, 1967). The framework for analysis comes during the study as the researcher tries to impose order on confusion. Frequent changes and adjustments are usually necessary to keep up with new data. Becker and Geer (1960) phrase field work in terms of a sequential process. They stress the efficacy of developing models of the system under study while the researcher is still gathering data. Then, consequent data collection takes its direction from the provisional models. In this way, successive models yield the final result, a "descriptive model best fitting" the experienced system.

In all, the exploratory approach to research emphasizes flexibility and openness. It is most appropriate when there are no a priori hypotheses available for testing, although Becker (1958) and Glaser and Strauss (1967) argue for a broader use. It only presupposes a desire to explore and experience an aspect of social reality with explicit future interests in mind. In this sense, the field study can be seen as a vehicle for the inductive development of new theory. This overall approach to data and theory is discussed in detail by Glaser and Strauss (1967).

The exploratory approach has a number of important limitations and drawbacks which must be kept in mind. Probably the most important contaminant is lack of detachment. In an exploratory field study, the investigator runs the risk of becoming so involved in the process that rather than being a nonparticipating observer, he may turn out to become a nonobserving participant (Whyte, 1955; Scott, 1965; Sellitz, et al., 1959). Also, conclusions cannot be confirmed without further experimental study and neither internal nor external criteria of validity are met. These criticisms, however, must be taken with a grain of salt, for they aim at targets not appropriate to the intended purposes of exploratory field work (Bruyn, 1963). The validity of the criticisms precludes exploratory results being used to test hypotheses or to test causality. The purpose of exploratory research, on the contrary, is only to evoke and develop insight and new hypotheses where none existed before. Thus, the question for field research is not how the information was obtained or how typical the organization studied is (methodology questions implied), but rather, how helpful the insights are or how the hypotheses developed fit reality. These questions can only be tested in more controlled and rigorous study (Glaser and Strauss, 1967). Sofer (1961:145) summarizes this position well

> It will be appreciated that the generalizations stated are based on retrospective study and not on the testing of hypotheses formally set up before field investigation and tested in a controlled manner capable of replication. This possibility is rare in all field studies. But, the claim made here is that the case studies lead to a deeper understanding of organizational change that can be checked against other intimate experiences with organizations and against new data which may be sought in studies more conventionally and rigorously organized and controlled.

The Becket study was carried out as an exploratory study tracing the process of change in an industrial glass plant over a little less than three years. Following the writings of Whyte (1955, 1951b), Guest (1962), Scott (1965), Gouldner (1954), and Walton (1972), the author has highlighted process of change over time. The study was not a "venture in validation" (Gouldner, 1954:247); instead, it was exploratory and, therefore, planned and adapted as the research was under way. The researcher had no initial hypotheses or research plan other than one of flexibility, openness, and a desire to understand. In the exploratory field tradition, the case comprises an effort to develop new insights and hypotheses concerning systematic organizational change. The basic concepts remained structural and behavioral in nature. The product was conjectures, open to falsification through experimental or experiential methods. In view of these scientificially primitive objectives, the writer must plainly describe the background to the study and the procedures used in gathering information (Glaser and Strauss, 1967; and Becker, 1958).

## FIELD METHODS

The research was carried out while the author was a research intern with the Boise Company. To gather as much data as possible, a number of complementary methods were used at Becket, a division of Boise. Extensive interviews were supplemented with observational data, documentary materials, and the use of what Whyte (1960) has called collaborators.

RESEARCH INTERN PROGRAM: In February 1971 an informal joint program was established between Carl Hoffman of the Boise Apparatus Company and the Organizational Behavior Department of the New York State School of Industrial and Labor Relations at Cornell University. The research intern program was to serve two purposes: to give a graduate student an opportunity to get field experience in an industrial organization and to provide the organizational development group at Boise with an extra person to do some long-desired research on the grid approach to organizational change. Hoffman was the consultant to the Becket plant for the grid program so that this original intership was to be related to Becket and the grid there. The only constraint was that the interning would be at the Becket plant. No other limits were set and the term of the internship was left to be determined.

After some negotiating with the plant manager, a very broad role was established for the intern. His task was to "trace the culture of the plant over time." With the upcoming grid program, this culturally oriented view was deemed appropriate. Nothing more specific was outlined. The exploratory, unstructured nature of the experience was considered best given the desire of the researcher for broad field experience and the overall scope of the intern idea. With agreement from Becket management, no restrictions were placed on the researcher except that the emphasis of his work was to be on monthly employees, excluding hourly workers since they were not involved in the grid program directly. It was made clear that the student was not working for the plant manager and was to be considered an extension of Hoffman. Intern records and notes were strictly private. The only promise made to the plant in return for its cooperation was a summary report at the end of the semester or summer. While there were a few early attempts by management to inquire into "what you are learning," these conflicts were quickly ironed out and further strengthened the intern's role as an independent observer.

Over the next six months there were thirty-four days of plant visits. A typical day would start at nine o'clock in the morning with a planning or manufacturing meeting, include three to four interviews, at least one other meeting, and a few tours around the plant, and would conclude about four thirty in the afternoon. While during the spring semester visits were regularly on Tuesdays, over the summer two visits a week were conducted on a random schedule. In all, ninety interviews were carried out. Thirty-five different men (88 percent of the monthly employees) were interviewed in all areas of the plant and throughout the whole managerial hierarchy. Forty-two formal and informal meetings were attended in all of the functional areas, and innumberable walks through the plant were made. Background data on productivity, performance records, and demographic records were collected where possible.

INTERVIEWS: The first few months of the research were devoted to establishing relationships with the men and further clarifying the intern role, rather than to directly gathering data (although this process of becoming known can be viewed as data itself). During this period interviews were designed to develop acquaintances; the format was relatively standardized and was aimed at putting the individual being interviewed at ease. It was hoped that the interviewee would leave the interview knowing enough about the intern, his work, and its purposes to satisfy the employee's curiosity and to reduce as much uncertainty as possible. Also, the interviews were to begin the process of developing increasing levels of trust and rapport between the men and the intern. If they also resulted in information on and a feel for the plant, all the better.

Interviews began with a reiteration and further clarification of the intern role, its independence from top management, and the confidentiality of the interview. Once this initial introduction (sometimes reintroduction) was completed, the interviewee could question the intern. Often there were questions about the intern's role, departmental major, education, and so on. This dialogue would often lead to personal divergences by the interviewee which were not cut short since they had a relaxing and loosening effect on the conversation.

Once these preliminaries were completed, the second part of the interview began with an open-ended question such as "Could you describe the basic operations of the plant and your function and duties in this process?" The response to this question would either suggest further areas to discuss or stimulate the interviewee to go on with a related story. The intern encouraged the interviewee to lead the conversation and only asked questions of the who, what, when, or where clarification variety. These initial unstructured interviews lasted between forty-five and sixty minutes.

The initial response throughout the plant was positive and cooperative, making it easy for the intern to meet and to interview formally men throughout the managerial hierarchy during the first few months at the plant. During this period rapport and acceptance were established with the most important men in the plant. This acceptance and its diffusion led to the development of a number of good relationships in all areas. During these first few months the intern also developed a feel for the plant as a technical and social system and he could soon understand the terms used on the floor and in the planning meetings. By the end of May, he could talk intelligently in most areas of plant concern.

The intern also became aware of the social dynamics within and between departments and of the influence of the "informal domain." This socialization process had a major influence on interviewing techniques. As he would begin to develop hypotheses or to integrate the "confusing welter of experiences," interviews became directed toward more specific areas. Thus, in the later stages of the research, the interviews became more focused and directed. Because of the relationships developed, quite direct questions could often be asked or hypotheses posed. At this stage, model-derived generalizations about the plant were put forth and the subject was asked to respond. Information obtained previously at Becket was used to push areas or to point out inconsistencies. Typically, these latter interviews lasted sixty to ninety minutes, longer than the normal introductory episodes.

During the whole research period and for both interview types, sessions were preferentially held in the interviewee's office or in a quiet area on the manufacturing floor. Usually, the interviewee was more relaxed behind his own desk or in his own territory. If he had no office or preferred to get away from his area, the intern's small office in the comptroller's area was available. There were a few other rules for this research: (A) The intern was neutral on all issues relating to the plant. Politics was also excluded. (B) The interviewer was nonevaluative and nonthreatening. A safe and supportive, yet interesting, atmosphere for discussions was created. (C) All interview notes were written up after the interview was completed either in the intern's office or that night at his home. In order to keep interpretations separate from observations, a notebook was reserved for all thoughts, opinions, and interpretations. Although this does not assure value-free notes, it is a step in the right direction. No pad was used during the interview because it might have hindered the intern's concentration on the conversation and because the plant personnel manager had warned of a suspicion of people walking around with a pad and pencil. (D) Language was also a consideration. Intellectual or overly academic words were avoided. Although the intern's speaking style depended on the interviewee, in general simple and direct words were used. (E) The plant was covered uniformly so that the intern was not identified with top management, the shift foreman, or any of the functional areas.

INFORMANTS: It became obvious early in the research that it was impossible to keep track of the plant with only one visit a week. For this reason a few reliable informants, or what Whyte (1960) has termed collaborators, were needed. Above the shift-foremen level a number of men were especially open, insightful, interested, and willing to enter into real discussions, often critical, of the plant. From this pool of men, collaborators were chosen using the following criteria: access to information, their ability to be trusted, and compatibility with the intern. Three collaborators, one at the manager level and two at the department-head level, were chosen.

These men were in separate functional areas of the plant and, therefore, they gave a good organizational perspective. Hypotheses and models were explained more openly to these men and their suggestions for further investigation were sought. They advised the intern of when and where interesting meetings would be held. At least one of these collaborators was visited on each trip to the plant and he would discuss the last week's events and suggest "something you'd be interested in today." At least once a month separate meetings to discuss the intern's current model would be held with informants. Besides helping build the model, the informants also read drafts of earlier summaries of the field experience and pointed out many factual errors in addition to giving their opinions of and suggestions on the model. Their insights, suggestions, and corrections were invaluable.

The intern attempted to develop one other atypical relationship at the plant. This was with the informal leader of the manufacturing floor, Dick Roe, who was recognized as the man in the plant most directly influential when it came to getting glass out the door and as the most influential man in the informal domain. Because of Roe's formal and informal influence and his potential effect on the research, the intern made a special effort to establish rapport and friendliness with him. Although Roe was not a collaborator as were the other three, the intern tried to see him as often.

OBSERVATIONS: The method used at Becket has been termed participant (Becker and Geer, 1960; Becker, 1958), unstructured, or nonsystematic observation (Scott, 1965; Sellitz *et al.*, 1959). Basic concerns of these observations were with the patterns of interactions and activities and their change over time. While most of the time was spent interviewing, at least one quarter of the day was spent either at meetings or touring the plant.

The observation strategy used at Becket can be separated into two areas for reasons similar to those discussed for interviewing. Initially the whole plant, its dynamics, and language were new and foreign. During the intern's initial few months, a large portion of time was spent attending planning, manufacturing, and other meetings in order to meet the men involved and pick up the language, problems, and processes of the organization. As hypotheses and models began to coalesce and the intern became familiar with the plant, observational activities became more directed. While the content of observations varied over time, the structure of the observational technique remained the same.

As many meetings as possible, ranging from formal reoccuring rituals to informal gatherings to one-of-a-kind crisis meetings, were attended. At these meetings the intern was passive and as unobtrusive as possible. He tried to arrive at meetings early and find an inconspicuous seat, usually away from the main table. Meeting behaviors and outcomes were a source of many insights and hypotheses. The reoccurring meetings were helpful in tracing observable changes over time. The crisis meetings were instructive in giving the observer the opportunity to watch behaviors in unplanned stressful conditions. These observed behaviors could be used as a fixed point in interview cross-checking.

On tours of the plant the intern could observe normal interactions and activities and could develop a feel for the plant as a whole, observing the technical system and the consequent relation between the various areas. While on the floor the intern could observe the impact of the technical system and could trace the many technical and physical changes. These walks also increased the intern's visibility in the plant and allowed him to run into people he would not normally see. On these walks interactions within and between areas were revealing: a shift foreman and engineer arguing over a piece of machinery, a department head supervising a piece of work, the plant manager interacting with workers on the floor, union-management arguments developing, and other day-to-day activity of a real-life organization were all noted.

DOCUMENTARY MATERIAL: The last source of information obtained from Becket was documentary materials, including newspaper clippings, interoffice memoranda, union contracts, and company reports. The company reports contained information on manning levels, productivity, union time, economic conditions, and other figures of plant performance.

The interoffice memos, the union newspaper, and the periodical notes posted in the plant were helpful in getting leads on problem areas, meeting times, company and plant changes, and union feelings. As a whole they were useful in getting a feeling for the culture of Boise and of Becket. The information from company reports such as productivity, manning levels, and economic indicators give the economic setting and the plant's performance over the three years involved in this study. The productivity figure is translated into net receipts per man hour, even though productivity as an indicator of plant performance can be misleading. At Becket, it is determined by the use of direct or indirect labor, engineering improvements, and sales volume. All of these changed at the plant. The figure of dollars per man hour, therefore, is partially confounded as an indicator of plant performance. Both sets of figures have been traced to 1969 and demographic data has been included. All information has been standardized except the demographic figures.

# Bibliography

Adams, Richard, and Jack Preiss
    1960    *Human Organization Research.* Homewood, Ill.: Dorsey.

Alderfer, Clayton
    1969    "Empirical Test of a New Theory of Human Needs." *Organizational Behavior and Human Performance* 4:142-149.

Arensberg, Conrad, and A. Niehoff.
    1964    *Introducing Social Change.* Chicago: Aldine.

Arensberg, Conrad, and Geoffry Tootel
    1957    "Plant Sociology: Real Discoveries and New Problems." In *Common Frontiers of the Social Sciences,* Mirra Komarovsky, ed., pp. 310-337. Chicago: Glenco Press.

Argyris, Chris
    1957    *Personality and Organization.* New York: Harper.
    1962    *Interpersonal Competence and Organizational Effectiveness.* Homewood, Ill.: Dorsey.
    1964    *Integrating the Individual and the Organization.* New York: Wiley.
    1965    *Organization and Innovation.* Homewood, Ill.: Dorsey.
    1969    "The Incompetence of Social Psychological Theory." *American Psychologist* 24(10):893-908.
    1971    *Management and Organizational Development.* New York: McGraw Hill.
    1973    "Personality and Organization Theory Revisited." *Administrative Science Quarterly* 18(2):141-167.

Back, Kurt
    1972    *Beyond Words,* New York: Russell Sage Foundation.

Barnes, Louis
    1967    "Organizational Change and Field Experiment Methods." In *Methods of Organizational Research,* Victor Vroom, ed., pp. 57-111. Pittsburgh: University of Pittsburgh Press.
    1969    "Approaches to Organizational Change." In *Planning of*

*Change,* Warren Bennis *et al.*, eds. 2nd ed. New York: Holt, Rinehart.

Becker, Howard
1958    "Problems of Inference and Proof in Participant Observation." *American Sociological Review* 23(6):652-660.

Becker, Howard, and Blanche Geer
1960    "Participant Observation: The Analysis of Qualitative Field Data." In *Human Organization Research,* Richard Adams and Jack Preiss, eds., pp. 267-289. Homewood, Ill.: Dorsey.

Beckhard, Richard
1969    *Organizational Development: Strategies and Models.* Reading, Mass.: Addison-Wesley.

Beckhard, Richard, and David Lake
1971    "Short Range Effects of a Team Development Effort." In *Social Intervention,* Harvey Hornstein *et al.,* eds., pp. 421-440. New York: Free Press.

Beer, Michael
1971    "Organizational Climate: Viewpoint from the Change Agent." Presented to Division 14, American Psychological Association Convention, Washington, D.C.
in press "The Technology of Organization Development." In *Handbook of Industrial and Organizational Psychology,* Marvin Dunnette, ed. Chicago: Rand McNally.

Beer, Michael, and Edgar Huse
1972    "A Systems Approach to Organization Development." *Journal of Applied Behavioral Science* 8:79-101.

Beer, Michael, and Steven Kleisath
1967    "Effects of the Managerial Grid Lab on Organizational Leadership Dimensions." Presented to Division 14, American Psychological Association Convention, Washington, D.C.

Bendix, Reinhard
1956    *Work and Authority in Industry.* New York: Wiley.

Bennis, Warren
1963    "New Role for the Behavioral Sciences: Effecting Organizational Change." *Administrative Science Quarterly* 8:125-137.
1966    *Changing Organizations.* New York: McGraw Hill.
1969    *Organizational Development.* Reading, Mass.: Addison-Wesley.

Bennis, Warren, Kenneth Benne, and Isedor Chin
1969    *The Planning of Change,* 2nd ed. New York: Holt Rinehart.

Blake, Robert, and Jane Mouton
1964    *The Managerial Grid.* Houston: Gulf.

Blake, Robert, *et al.*
1964    "Breakthrough in Organizational Development." *Harvard Business Review* 42:135-148.

Blau, Peter
1955    *Dynamics of Bureaucracy.* Chicago: University of Chicago Press.

Bowers, Dave
1973    "O.D. Techniques and Their Results in 23 Organizations." *Journal of Applied Behavioral Science* 9:21-44.

Bruyn, Severyn
1963    "Methodology of Participant Observation." *Human Organizations* 22(3):224-230.

Buchanan, Paul
1969    "Laboratory Training and Organizational Development." *Administrative Science Quarterly* 14:466-480.

Burns, Thomas, and George Stalker
1961    *The Management of Innovation.* London: Tavistock.

Cadwell, Raymond
1970    *Barriers to Planned Change.* Dublin: Irish National Productivity Committee.

Campbell, Donald, and Julian Stanley
1963    *Experimental and Quasi-Experimental Designs for Research.* Chicago: Rand McNally.

Campbell, John
1971    "Personnel Training and Development." In *Annual Review of Psychology*, Paul Mussen and Mark Rosenzweig, eds. 22:565-603. Palo Alto: American Review.

Campbell, John, *et al.*
1970    *Managerial Behavior, Performance, and Effectiveness.* New York: McGraw Hill.

Campbell, John, and Marvin Dunnette
1968    "Effectiveness of T Group Experiences in Managerial Training and Development." *Psychological Bulletin* 70:73-108.

Cannell, Charles, and Robert Kahn
1969    "Interviewing." In *Handbook of Social Psychology*, Gardner Lindzey and Eliot Aronson, eds. 2:Chap. 15. 2nd ed. Reading, Mass.: Addison-Wesley.

Chapple, Eliot, and Leonard Sayles
1961    *The Measure of Management.* New York: MacMillan.

Coch, L., and J.R. French
1948    "Overcoming Resistance to Change." *Human Relations* 1:512-533.

Emery, Fred, and Eric Trist
1965    "The Causal Texture of Organizational Environments." *Human Relations* 18:21-32.

Etzioni, Amitai
1961    *Comparative Analysis of Complex Organizations.* New York: Free Press.
1964    *Modern Organizations.* Englewood Cliffs, N.J.: Prentice Hall.

Fayol, Henri
1949    *General and Industrial Management.* New York: Pitman.

French, Wendell, and Cecil Bell.
1973    *Organization Development.* Englewood, N.J.: Prentice Hall.

Friedlander, Frank
1967    "Impact of Organizational Training Laboratories Upon the Effectiveness and Interaction of Ongoing Work Groups." *Personnel Psychology* 20(3):289-308.

Galbreith, Jay
1969    "Organizational Design: An Information Processing View." Working Paper no. 425-69. Cambridge: Sloan School, Massachusetts Institute of Technology.
1973    *Designing Complex Organizations.* Reading, Mass.: Addison-Wesley.

Glaser, Barney, and Auslem Strauss
1967    *The Discovery of Grounded Theory.* Chicago: Aldine.

Gardner, John
1964    *Self Renewal.* New York: Harper.

Golembiewski, Robert
1964    "Authority as a Problem in Overlays." *Administrative Science Quarterly* 9(1):22-49.

Golembiewski, Robert, and Stokes Carrigan
1970    "Persistance of Laboratory Induced Changes in Organizational Styles." *Administrative Science Quarterly* 15(3):330-341.

Gouldner, Alvin
1954    *Patterns of Industrial Bureaucracy.* New York: Free Press.

Greiner, Larry
    1967    "Patterns of Organizational Change." *Harvard Business Review*
            45:119-131.
    1972    "Evolution and Revolution in Organizational Development."
            Unpublished manuscript, Cambridge: Harvard University
            Graduate School of Business Administration.

Guest, Robert
    1962    *Organizational Change*. Homewood, Ill.: Dorsey.

Hage, Jerald, and Mike Aiken
    1969    "Routine Technology, Social Structure, and Organizational
            Goals." *Administrative Science Quarterly* 14(3):366-378.
    1970    *Social Change in Complex Organizations*. New York: Random
            House.

Hall, Calvin, and Gardner Lindzey
    1970    *Theories of Personality*. 2nd ed. New York: Wiley.

Hall, Edward, and Khalil Nougaim
    1968    "Examination of Maslow's Need Hierarchy: An Organiza-
            tional Setting." *Organizational Behavior and Human Perform-
            ance* 3:12-35.

Harrison, Roger
    1962    "Impact of the Laboratory on Perceptions of Others by the
            The Experimental Group." In *Interpersonal Competence and
            Organizational Effectiveness,* Chris Argyris, ed., pp. 261-271.
            Homewood, Ill.: Irwin.

Heller, Frank
    1970    "Group Feedback Analysis as a Change Agent." *Human
            Relations* 23(4):319-334.

Herzberg, Frederick
    1966    *Work and the Nature of Man*. New York: World.

Holmberg, Alan
    1960    "The Research and Development Approach to Change." In
            *Human Organization Research*, Richard Adams and Jack Preiss,
            eds., pp. 76-89. Homewood, Ill.: Dorsey.

Homans, George
    1950    *The Human Group*. New York: Harcourt Brace.

Hornstein, Harvey, *et al.*
    1971    *Social Intervention: A Behavioral Science Approach*. New York:
            MacMillan.

Huse, Edgar, and Michael Beer
1971    "Eclectic Appraoch to O.D." *Harvard Business Review* 29(5):103-112.

Jahoda, Marie, Martin Deutsch, and Stuart Cook
1951    *Research Methods in Social Relations.* New York: Dryden.

Jaques, Eliot
1951    *The Changing Culture of a Factory.* London: Tavistock.

Kahn, Robert, *et al.*
1964    *Organizational Stress.* New York: Wiley.

Kahn, Robert, and Charles Cannell
1957    *Dynamics of Interviewing.* New York: Wiley.

Katz, David, and Robert Kahn
1966    *Social Psychology of Organizations.* New York: Wiley.

Kegan, Daniel
1971    "Organization Development: Description, Issues, and Research Results." *Academy of Management Journal* 14:453-464.

Kolb, David, and A. Frohman
1970    "An Organizational Development Approach to Consulting." *Sloan Management Review* 12:51-66.

Kolb, David, Irwin Rubin, and J. MacIntyre
1970    *Organizational Psychology: An Experiential Approach.* Englewood Cliffs, N.J.: Prentice Hall.

Kreinik, William, and Robert Colarelli
1971    "Managerial Grid Training for Mental Hospital Personnel." *Human Relations* 24(1):91-104.

Kuhn, Thomas
1962    *Structure of Scientific Revolutions.* Chicago: University of Chicago Press.

Lachenmeyer, Charles
1970    "Experimentation: a Misunderstood Methodology in Psychological Research." *American Psychologist* 25: 617-624.

Lake, Dale, Martin Ritvo, and George O'Brien
1969    "Applying Behavioral Science: Current Projects." *Journal of Applied Behavioral Science* 5(3):367-392.

Lawrence, Paul
1958    *The Changing of Organizational Behavior Patterns.* Boston: Riverside.

Lawrence, Paul, and Jay Lorsch
1967    *Organization and Environment.* Cambridge: Harvard University Press.
1969    *Developing Organizations.* Reading, Mass.: Addison-Wesley.

Leavitt, Harold
1965    "Applied Organizational Change In Industry." In *Handbook of Organizations,* James March, ed., pp. 1144-1170. Chicago: Rand McNally.

Lewin, Kurt
1958    "Group Decision and Social Change." In *Readings in Social Psychology,* Eleanor Maccoby *et al.,* eds., pp. 197-211. 3rd ed. New York: Holt.

Likert, Rensis
1961    *New Patterns of Management.* New York: McGraw Hill.
1967    *The Human Organization.* New York: McGraw Hill.

Liebow, Elliot
1967    *Tally's Corner.* Boston: Little Brown Co.

Lippitt, Gordon
1969    *Organizational Renewal.* New York: Meredith.

Lippitt, Ronald, James Watson, and Bruce Westley
1958    *The Dynamics of Planned Change.* New York: Harcourt Brace.

McGrath, Joseph
1964    "Towards a Theory of Method for Research on Organization." In *New Perspectives in Organizational Research,* William Cooper *et al.,* eds., pp. 533-576. New York: Wiley.

McGregor, Douglas
1960    *The Human Side of Enterprise.* New York: McGraw Hill.

Maisse, Joseph
1965    "Management Theory." In *Handbook of Organizations,* James March, ed., pp. 387-423. Chicago: Rand McNally.

Mann, Floyd, and Frank Neff
1961    *Managing Major Change in Organizations.* Ann Arbor: Foundation for Research on Human Behavior.

March, James, ed.
1965    *Handbook of Organizations.* Chicago: Rand McNally.

March, James, and Herbert Simon
1958    *Organizations.* New York: Wiley.

Marrow, Alfred, David Bowers, and Stanley Seashore
1967    *Management by Participation.* New York: Harper.

Maslow, Abraham
  1962    *Toward a Psychology of Being.* New York: Van Nostrand.
  1965    *Eupsychian Management.* Homewood, Ill.: Irwin.

Michael, Donald
  1970    "On the Social Psychology of Organizational Resistance to Long Range Planning." Paper presented at symposium on Technology in Organizations of the Future, at the New York State School of Industrial and Labor Relations, Cornell University.

Mohr, Lawrence
  1971    "Organizational Technology and Organizational Structure." *Administrative Science Quarterly* 16(2):444-459.

Morse, Nancy, and Everett Reimer
  1956    "Experimental Change of a Major Organizational Variable." *Journal of Abnormal Social Psychology* 52(2):120-129.

Mouzelis, Nicos
  1967    *Organizations and Bureaucracy.* Chicago: Aldine.

Nagel, Ernst
  1961    *The Structure of Science.* New York: Harcourt Brace.

Perrow, Charles
  1970    *Organizational Analysis: A Sociological View.* Belmont, Calif.: Wadsworth.
  1972    *Complex Organizations.* Glenview, Ill.: Scott, Foresman.

Phillips, Kevin
  1971    *Knowledge From What?* Chicago: Rand McNally.

Pugh, P.S.
  1966    "Modern Organizational Theory." *Psychological Bulletin* 66(4):235-251.

Rice, A.K.
  1958    *Productivity and Social Organization.* London: Tavistock.

Richardson, Stephen, Barbara Dohrenwend, and David Klein
  1965    *Interviewing.* New York: Basic Books.

Rubin, Irwin
  1967    "Reduction of Prejudice Through Laboratory Training." *Journal of Applied Behavioral Science* 3(1):29-50.

Sayles, Leonard
  1962    "Change Process in Organizations: An Applied Anthropological Analysis." *Human Organizations* 21(2):62-67.

Schein, Edgar
  1970    *Organizational Psychology*. 2nd ed. Englewood Cliffs, N.J.:
          Prentice Hall.

Schein, Edgar, and Warren Bennis
  1965    *Personnel and Organizational Change Through Group Methods*.
          New York: Wiley.

Scott, William
  1963    "Field Work in Formal Organizations." *Human Organizations*
          22(2):162-168.
  1965    "Field Methods in the Study of Organizations." In *Handbook
          of Organizations*, James March, ed., pp. 261-304. Chicago:
          Rand McNally.

Seashore, Stanley, and David Bowers
  1963    *Changing the Structure and Functioning of an Organization*. Ann
          Arbor: University of Michigan Press.
  1970    "Durability of Organizational Change." *American Psychologist*
          25:227-230.

Sellitz, Claire, *et al.*
  1959    *Research Methods in Social Relations*. Rev. ed. New York: Holt
          Rinehart.

Shepard, Herbert
  1965    "Changing Interpersonal and Inter-Group Relationships in
          Organizations," In *Handbook of Organizations*, James March,
          ed., pp. 1115-1144. Chicago: Rand McNally.

Shepard, Herbert, and Robert Blake
  1962    "Changing Behavior Through Cognitive Change." *Human
          Organizations* 21(2):88-96.

Shimmin, Sylvia
  1971    "Behavior in Organizations." *Occupational Psychology:*
          25(1):13-27.

Sofer, Cyril
  1959    *Organization from Within*. London: Tavistock.

Steele, Fred
  1971    "Physical Settings and Organizational Development." In
          *Social Intervention*, Harvey Hornstein *et al.*, eds., pp. 244-254.
          New York: Free Press.

Strauss, George
  1964    "Some Notes on Power Equalization." Reprint 225. Berkeley:
          Institute of Industrial Relations, University of California.

Taylor, Frederic W.
1911    *Principles of Scientific Management*. New York: Harper.

Taylor, James
1971    *Technology and Planned Organizational Change*. Ann Arbor: University of Michigan Press.

Thompson, James
1967    *Organizations in Action*. New York: McGraw Hill.

Toffler, Alvin
1970    *Future Shock*. New York: Random House.

Trist, Eric, and William Bamforth
1951    "Some Social and Psychological Consequences of the Long Wall Method of Coal Getting." *Human Relations* 4:3-38.

Tushman, Michael
1971    "Towards a Contingency Method of Inquiry." Manuscript. Ithaca: New York State School of Industrial and Labor Relations, Cornell University.

Udy, Stanley
1965    "The Comparative Analysis of Organizations." In *Handbook of Organizations,* James March, ed., pp. 678-710. Chicago: Rand McNally.

U.S. Department of Health, Education and Welfare
1973    *Work in America*. Cambridge: Massachusetts Institute of Technology.

Vroom, Victor, ed.
1967    *Methods of Organizational Research*. Pittsburgh: University of Pittsburgh Press.

Walton, Richard
1972    "Advantages and Attributes of the Case Study." *Journal of Applied Behavioral Science* 8:72-78.

Webb, Eugene, *et al.*
1966    *Unobstrusive Measures: Non-Reactive Measures in Social Sciences*. Chicago: Rand McNally.

Weick, Karl
1969    *Social Psychology of Organizing*. Reading, Mass.: Addison-Wesley.

Weiss, Robert and Martin Rein
1970    "The Evaluation of Broad-Aim Programs." *Administrative Science Quarterly* 25:97-109.

Weschler, Irving, and Edgar Schein
  1962   *Issues in Training*. Washington, D.C.: National Training Laboratories.

Whyte, William F.
  1951a  *Pattern for Industrial Peace*. New York: Harper.
  1951b  "Observational Field Work Methods." In *Research Methods in Social Relations*. Marie Jahoda *et al*. eds., 2:493-513. New York: Dryden.
  1955   *Street Corner Society*. Enlarged ed. Chicago: University of Chicago Press.
  1960   "Interviewing in Field Research." In *Human Organization Research*, Richard Adams and Jack Preiss, eds., pp. 352-374.
  1971   "Changing the Power Structure on the Countryside." Paper given during ILR 623, New York State School of Industrial and Labor Relations, Cornell University.

Winn, Alexander
  1969   "The Laboratory Approach to Organizational Development." *Journal of Management Studies* 6:155-166.

Wohlking, Wallace
  1971   "Management Training: Where Has It Gone Wrong?" *Training and Development Journal* 25(1):1-6.

Woodward, Joan
  1965   *Industrial Organizations*. London: Oxford University Press.

Zaleznick, Abraham
  1965   "Interpersonal Relations in Organizations." In *Handbook of Organizations*, James March, ed., pp. 574-614. Chicago: Rand McNally.

# AUTHOR INDEX